ADVANCE PRAISE

"Kids may not come with an instruction manual, but now home office parenting does! Successful entrepreneur, Jennifer Kalita, hits one out of the park with this humorous, thoughtful, and soulful manual for anyone who wants practical, immediate strategies for how to realistically integrate a business into your home and your life as a parent.

Funny and insightful, *The Home Office Parent* is more than just a playbook for the joyful co-mingling of laptops and lollipops; it is a powerful business tool that shares the secrets to success for entrepreneurs who refuse to trade in their lives for their work.

If you have a home office or kids or both, this book is a must-read! Finally, someone tells us how to sustain happy kids and happy clients...the REAL bottom line."

Suzi Pomerantz, CEO, Executive Coach, & Author, *Seal the Deal: The Essential Mindsets for Growing Your Professional Services Business*, www.sealthedealbook.com

"I was thrilled to read a book that validates the home office parent. As powerful contributors to the business community, this segment is increasingly becoming a force to be reckoned with. Yet, with that success comes many questions and concerns about blending, balancing, and honoring our commitment as parents, spouses and friends. In this book, Jennifer Kalita manages to empower us with sound professional advice without sacrificing the parenthood part of the equation as so many other how-to books tend to do. Thank you for providing "real-deal" solutions for both the new and seasoned home office parent."

Beth Smith, Senior Editor, *Hybrid Mom* Magazine
www.hybridmom.com

"*The Home Office Parent* takes a realistic look at the challenges facing work-at-home parents of young children. One of the most compelling points in the book is the understanding that young children need their parents' emotional presence, not just their physical presence, and Jennifer Kalita offers advice on how to achieve this. Children are about relationships, and they don't easily understand business or the work stresses their parents may face. Jennifer shows empathy for both home office parents and their young children.

This book offers a number of helpful survival strategies. One key tip she discusses is the importance of establishing clear parameters for yourself and others so as to eliminate confusion over roles, expectations and needs. In 25 years of early childhood development work, we've witnessed a growing understanding of the importance of a child's first years. Now, home-office parents have a guide to help them support these early years and achieve success in their businesses."

Ginger Ward, MA Ed., Founder & CEO
The Arizona Institute for Early Childhood Development
www.swhd.org

"*The Home Office Parent* is written with warmth, love and tremendous knowledge. Jennifer Kalita exudes confidence for entrepreneurs who want to parent and maintain a professional life with grace. Even if you have to read it in the bathroom, you must do so if you want to be proficient in both arenas of your life."

Dotsie Bregel, Founder, National Association of Baby Boomer Women
www.nabbw.com

"Well done! As a recovering corporate executive turned home office parent, this book couldn't have come at a better time. Everything Jennifer Kalita writes is dead on. I felt like maybe she'd been to my house.

Many of us turn to entrepreneurship to have more freedom and balance, only to find ourselves out of control and spending less quality time with our families. To feel torn between being a great parent and a successful business person is common. Thankfully, Jennifer delivers a book that we can relate to, reminds us that we have choices, and provides techniques and tools to make it all possible. She reminds us that we can have it all, but not all at once.

This book is also a quick read, so you get the information you need in a very concise format."

"This book should be required reading for every parent who is thinking about starting a business, and every entrepreneur who is thinking about starting a family. I wish I'd had it when I started my company! This fun-to-read book decodes the mystery of trying to do two important things very well. I especially love the chapter-ending "Key Concepts" that are easy to reference long after you've read the book. And believe me, you'll want to go back to this book periodically for a sanity check!"

"Jennifer Kalita's wonderful book fills a niche for the stay-at-home parent who also works from home. Written in a straight-forward manner with a touch of humor and using examples any parent will appreciate, *The Home Office Parent* offers sound advice and practical strategies for those brave enough to tackle balancing a home-based business with staying home full-time."

Karen Steede Terry, Author, *Full-Time Woman, Part-Time Career*
www.fulltimewoman.com

"This book hits a home run, which is good news for all the moms and dads out there who are balancing family and home-based work. Jennifer Kalita, with a voice of experience, takes a laser-sharp focus on the critical issues of achieving success from a home office. Without being an effective parent, even achieving great success in business will lose its meaning.

Quick, get your copy and read it now! Your spouse, your co-workers—and most importantly—your kids will thank you. And you'll be both glad and prosperous."

Debra A. Dinnocenzo, President, Virtual Works!, Author, *101 Tips for Telecommuters* and *Working Too Much Can Make You Grumpy*
www.virtualworkswell.com

"*The Home Office Parent* is full of sound, practical advice. Each challenge of this lifestyle is examined and then invaluable strategies are presented to manage those challenges. This book should be read by every home office parent...and her/his spouse!"

Nancy Daniel, Founder & President, Moms, Inc.
www.momsinc.org

"*The Home Office Parent* is full of insight on what it's really like and what it truly takes to balance the demands of work and family. Take this book's advice seriously. I'm going to be setting up some better boundaries and spend less time waving my hands in the air and acting frustrated as a result.

Life's too short, and Jennifer Kalita hits the nail on the head with her real world experience. We can all benefit from this book's ability to help us become better "entrepren-OREOs" too. My kids don't know it, but they should be grateful for this book!"

Beth Sanders, Founder & CEO, LifeBio
www.lifebio.com

"Jennifer Kalita forces you to truly look at the issues and the support that you need, and recognize that although you can be a parent and run a business, certain things need to give in order for you to do either of these jobs well.

The Home Office Parent forces you to look inside yourself and come up with your views on extremely thought provoking topics such as your definition of success, your goals and timing on achieving them, and how you can establish boundaries and achieve success while you work at home. Jennifer is brutally honest in her truths about how others will perceive you as a stay-at-home parent with a hobby or "side business" as opposed to a business person who has some extremely busy days.

Jennifer speaks from experience, and although the truth isn't always pretty, she is able to lay everything out in a detailed and easy to read format with questions, summaries and "survival strategies" at the end of each chapter. *The Home Office Parent* is a quick read (because who has time to really sit and read a book?) and a must read for all parents who currently are or contemplating becoming home office parents."

Amy Platt, Owner & Founder, LIParentSource
www.liparentsource.com

"Most books written by home office parents aren't FOR home office parents. Sure, you catch a glimpse of their struggles as they wipe away peanut butter from their keyboard while typing the next line. You get a vague sense of their concurrent chaos, but you never get the full-blown picture or a recipe for how they overcome their condition to move beyond survival to sustainable success. Lucky for us, Jennifer Kalita does.

This brilliant writer provides home office parents with a practical guide to home office parenthood. Her tone is real, her advice true. I found myself acknowledged within the first pages of her book. Being a home-based businesswoman with small children, I was on the writer's side from the moment I cracked the cover. Her witty, smart writing reeled me in and I was hers the moment she claimed home office parenting is a synergistic lifestyle assembled with tears, temporary insanity, mind-numbing tedium and a full-blown case of mutual respect, which is the basis of the entire operation.

For anyone who wants to shout out 'Just because I'm home doesn't mean I'm available,' they will find themselves in this book. Even better, they will find a way to improve their best practices to return to the joy borne of their decision to work from home in the first place. I highly recommend this book to anyone who's ever thought working from home would be a cakewalk."

Christine Louise Hohlbaum, Author, *Diary Of A Mother* and *SAHM I Am: Tales of a Stay-at-Home Mom in Europe*
www.diaryofamother.com

"This book is a must for **_anyone_** contemplating starting their own home based business...taking you step by step to achieve your goal of leading a balanced life while still achieving excellence at home and at work.

Starting a home based business can seem overwhelming on top of your current responsibilities, but *The Home Office Parent* provides a framework and tools to help you:

- Create a plan that assesses and draws in the necessary support;
- Manage the expectations associated with each of your many hats;
- Set up sanity checks for you and your support structure; and
- Implement flexible boundaries that will enable you to excel in all of your roles without requiring super human strength or marathon days.

A quick read, this book frankly discusses the realities of working from home and has the tools to help you overcome the obstacles and ensure long-term success."

Colleen Contreras, PMP & Author, *Build the Life You Want AND Still Have Time to Enjoy It!*
www.momentum2execution.com

"*The Home Office Parent* is at once both a very practical must-read for those considering becoming home office parents, and a good wake-up call for those of us who have been doing it so long that we sometimes slip into imbalance between the home office and the parenting. Jennifer Kalita doesn't delve into the rudimentary "how-to furnish the office" issues, but rather guides the reader through ways to assess his or her own strengths and weaknesses to set up the business—not just the space in which it exists.

This is not a feel-good pep-talk advocating that everyone abandon the commute to become a home office parent. It looks at the lifestyle from every part of the equation and provides valuable information to help you make the decision and stay on a (mostly) sane course when you have. Jennifer prepares the reader for the realities so they can make the decision with open eyes to, or not to, take on this lifestyle change."

Cynthia L. McVey, APR, CEO, Cindy Lee Associates
www.cindyleepr.com

"As a member of Jennifer Kalita's target audience, I found that this book spoke honestly, succinctly and directly. It is extremely well organized and with humor peppered throughout, very easy and enjoyable to read.

This is a terrific book for someone thinking about starting a home based business, before or after children are in the picture, and is just as beneficial to someone already in the throes of a home based business/parenting situation.

I found the "Successful Life Weekly Action Plans" to be particularly helpful. "Key Concepts" at the end of each chapter summarize and help the reader retain, or at least reference later, the information. The author also understands and takes into account that not one way works for everyone and the "Success Exercises" at the end of each chapter truly help each reader individually, hence the personalized nature of the book. This fact sets this book apart from others like it.

This is a book that I will keep, recommend to others and reference in the future."

Vanessa Richardson, Illustrator, VR Illustration
www.vrillustration.com

THE
HOME OFFICE
PARENT

How to Raise Kids & Profits
Under One Roof

Jennifer Kalita

Wyatt-MacKenzie Publishing, Inc.
DEADWOOD, OREGON

The Home Office Parent: How to Raise
Kids & Profits Under One Roof by Jennifer Kalita

ISBN: 978-1-932279-68-9

©2007, Jennifer Kalita

Library of Congress Control Number: 2006935778

Edited by Felicia M. Barlow

Published by The Mom-Writers Publishing Cooperative
Wyatt-MacKenzie Publishing, Inc., Deadwood, OR
www.WyMacPublishing.com (541) 964-3314

Requests for permission or further information should be addressed to:
Wyatt-MacKenzie Publishing, 15115 Highway 36,
Deadwood, Oregon 97430

Printed in the United States of America

Dedication

For Ba, without whom there would be nothing to write

Table of Contents

Acknowledgements

When I finish reading a book, I always flip back to the author's acknowledgements section, because I want to know more about the writer's journey. Who supported this author throughout the process? Who played what role in taking this book from the musings of one individual all the way to a cohesive, bound, tangible collection of thoughts?

As a busy home office parent, I also like to know who helped these writers to carve out the time needed to bring forth a book. Many people have fantastic ideas in their heads, but not necessarily the time and space to write or publish them. As I am blessed to have the professional support and personal encouragement that makes the writing and publishing process worth the ride, I'd like to acknowledge the enormous contribution that so many have made on the road leading up to this book.

While many writers end a section like this with thanks to their families, this is instead where I must begin. My husband, Ba, has taught me what unconditional love and unwavering support feel like, and from those two things stem all else. I can freely put myself, my work and my book out there in the big world because I have already achieved the ultimate success in partnering with him. His compassion makes me more tolerant. His intelligence keeps me engaged. His calm enables me to live a balanced life at a reasonable pace. His humor will most certainly give me laugh lines. Because of his love for and belief in me, I have the opportunity to share what I've learned on the home office parenting obstacle course that he and I have stumbled through together on the pages of this book. My gratitude and appreciation for him are immeasurable. Thank you, my love.

Without my daughters, Diane and Megan, there would simply be no book—and so little joy. Without the opportunity to parent and learn from them, I would have no input on this subject. To call them "beautiful" or "amazing" or "wonderful" seems so inadequate when describing how profoundly they have affected my life and my work. Their insights are too wise for their small bodies; their hearts too giving and generous at what are the typically self-involved ages of six and three. They challenge me to be consistent and to honor the commitment of being the mom they need me to be. They teach me to be more compassionate and understanding, and to laugh every chance I get. I am grateful to them for being proud of my work instead of resenting it for sometimes taking me away from them. I am at once humbled and fortified by their love and respect, and I am proud to call them my daughters. Thank you, my little lambs.

My family has played such a significant role in teaching me that tough circumstances in childhood don't have to lead to a difficult life in adulthood. I am grateful to my maternal grandparents, Paul and Mary, who raised me and taught me what love, loyalty, and Italian cooking can bring to your life. I am inspired by Aunt Ann, who taught me to stretch and grow and use every talent God gave me to the fullest (and not to wait for the permission of others to do so). For my sense of independence and my ability to stand up for myself, I am most grateful to Paul. And for Jess; you are not my sister by chance, but by choice.

I was also blessed to inherit the instant and genuine love of my husband's parents, Chabi and Minoti, who showed me that sometimes you get your ideal Mommy and Daddy a little later in life. I'm so thankful for Anji, my sister-in-law, who strikes the balance between being a powerful businesswoman and a loving sister at every turn. And our extended family would be lost without Auntie Lois-Ellen, whose enveloping love binds us all across the miles and whom I admire and respect beyond words. Dearest Auntie, you are whom I hope to be when I grow up.

The hectic pace of any home office parent can make for one tired author. I am revived by Aunt Peachie, whose loving perspective, nurturing spirit and relentless sense of humor keep me going. For my brother Carl, who refuses to entertain the notion that I am capable of anything less than world domination, I am challenged by your vision and thankful for your love. And for my cousin Christopher...whatever room you're in, that is home to me.

"Good friends are the family you create," as the saying goes, and I am so blessed to have created a truly beautiful second family. Without Mike and Kim Billok, this would be a very different book, and a much less joyous life. Home office parents need support and understanding and laughter and...well, a wine break sometimes. Thank you for being all of that and more. And for Kim's parents, Ed and Della Latta, you both exemplify the character and integrity I aspire to. Thank you for always having a place for me at your table.

For Felicia Barlow, who was not just the editor of this book, but who continues to be a true and beautiful source of love and light in my life. Thank you for removing the greatest obstacle I faced in writing this content, simply by reframing the challenge for me.

Thanks to Terilee Harrison, author of *The Business Mom Guide Book*, who introduced me to Wyatt-MacKenzie Publishing and of course, to Nancy Cleary, my patient publisher and fellow home office parent. I appreciate your support of women writers and your belief in me.

I am grateful to all of the home office parents who shared their stories with me, as it is in sharing the struggle, not touting the victory, that we truly empower each other.

Lastly, I am motivated by the memory and beautiful spirit of my mother, Diane. Our time together on this earth was brief, but our connection is lasting.

Wishing you a life in business and in balance,
Jennifer

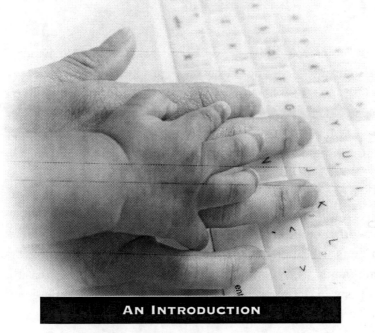

AN INTRODUCTION

Laptops & Licorice & Lunacy...Oh My

You've read the books on how to set up a successful home business, written by the business experts. You've read the books on parenting, published by the psychology experts. Now, here's the book about where the two meet—and often, collide.

I write this book knowing two things to be true: I am a successful home-based businesswoman, but, more important, I am a successful parent. I know this because I have both clients and children who know they have value and that I do, too.

I write this book from the trenches—the often loud and chaotic trenches—and I only wish someone had published a book like this for me years ago. During my initial foray into home office parenting, I found a few books about how to create the best home-based business; other books that were basically reference material about how to set up home-based office systems; and still others that were comprised of numerous home office parent case studies. But nowhere did I find a concrete plan of action for home office parenting success. So, like all good entrepreneurs, I saw a need and filled it.

This comprehensive guide to becoming a sane home office parent is based on real experiences—mine, and those of numerous other home office moms and dads. While many home office parents will find this information helpful in creating the work and family life they know is possible, I'll caution you that the honesty in this book may completely turn you off of the home office parenting arrangement altogether.

Either way, this author's goal is to give you the information and tools that will help you to design the optimal situation for you and your family. Your choice may or may not include home office parenting, but reading this book will give you the truth behind the increasingly popular transition that parents are making to raise kids and profits under the same roof.

While the advice in this book can be applied to the needs of all home office parents, it is specifically geared toward home office parents with young children who don't yet attend school on a full-time basis. These professionals have unique needs, as it is their challenge to be full-time parents and business managers...and do both well.

Add to this that home office parents are often confused with being stay-at-home parents, which only compounds their frustration. One choice is no better or worse than the other, but there's a big difference between working at home as a full-time parent, and working at home as a home office parent.

You get all of the calls to pick relatives up at the airport. You're forever expected to drop what you're doing at a moment's notice by the people in your life who don't understand that you do, in fact, work. You will be asked to chair the committee at your church or coach soccer at your son's pre-school because, after all, "you're at home."

Throughout the book, you'll explore this and other issues few entrepreneurs or telecommuters thoroughly confront before diving in to become home office parents. You'll look at defining and living what often feel like conflicting roles as a parent and a professional. You'll learn how to prioritize and set boundaries that actually work, which is more difficult than it may at first sound.

I'll show you how to get (and keep) the help you need, get organized, and achieve balance between a home office and a home life. And, of course, we'll take a sneak peak into the psyches of the caregivers and spouses who are directly affected by your choices.

I've included self-coaching exercises at the end of each chapter in order to help you take the ideas from the book, evaluate how they play out for you, and instantaneously apply them to your own life. So, to get the most out of the concepts on the pages that follow, pour a glass of your favorite concoction, find a comfortable chair or sofa, grab a notebook, and locate a pen with ink before you start reading.

I won't bother you with the latest statistics on how many home office parents start businesses everyday, because the growth is so exponential that any statistic will be out of date before this book is printed. As a matter of fact, the reported data changed twice in the year that I wrote this book. But think about it for a minute...you probably have at least one home office parent in your family or circle of friends, if not several.

Statistics aside, we all know that thanks to the Internet, home-based enterprises are on the rise, and this book is written primarily for those entrepreneurs. The advice and techniques for success, however, can certainly be applied to telecommuters, as more employees than ever are working virtually from their home offices in an effort to cut corporate overhead.

And dads, never fear. This is not a book for mommies only. The advice and survival strategies you'll find throughout these pages are specific only to the controlled chaos that all home office parents, regardless of gender, call their lives.

While I did not conduct formal interviews with the most successful home office parents for this book, I did document my own successes and less-than-successes; I don't say *failures* because that would communicate a loss, or a falling down and staying down. Since I got back up, and learned so much from the experiences, *failures* just doesn't describe things accurately or do the journey any justice.

I also listened to my colleagues as they struggled to find their identities beneath piles of faxes and scribbled coloring book pages (a.k.a. "hang up with your client and pay attention to me" directives). I let them vent about their customers, curse their hard drives, damn the printer straight to hell, and wonder how in the name of all that is decent and holy they were going to pull this whole home office thing off.

Then I listened some more (and laughed out loud) when they regaled me with stories of how their kids threw up on the fax machine; yelled "I flushed AND wiped!" during the most inopportune, big-fat-client-on-the-phone moment; and colored on presentation graphics to "make them pretty."

But I really heard them when they grew quieter, reflecting on what their home office work lives were costing them personally. The not-so-funny stories, like when little Sam dropped his chin to his chest and shuffled out of Dad's office because Dad was "right in the middle of something," or when young Sarah started to cry because they weren't going to the park after all...even after she'd been such a good sport about Mom saying "just give me one more minute" about twenty times as she hovered over her laptop.

I gave advice when asked, support when needed, but most often, I just listened. And together we reached the good stuff in the end...the thing they learned; the strategy they employed; the new boundary they established. And that is how this book came to be.

As with any endeavor, it's simply practical to have a "how-to" guide at your disposal as you embark on—or muddle through—the journey. Whether you're considering working from home, you already do, or you're ready to give up on the whole thing because you feel like you're failing your family, yourself, and the global economy—read on.

And here's the really good news: you no longer have to choose between being a good professional and a good parent. Now, you can excel at being the best home office parent on the block.

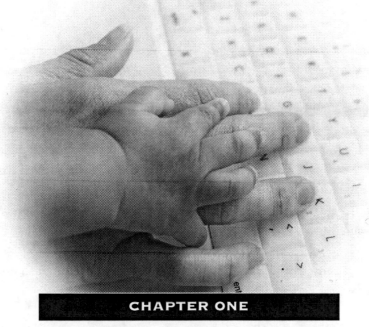

CHAPTER ONE

The Reason & Reality
Behind the Choice

Chances are that your decision to become a home-based business owner was a well-thought out one. Despite vast and fast entrepreneurial growth, very few people just fall into something like this, as it takes a great deal of spirit, tenacity and vision.

If you're anything like me, your decision to create a home-based enterprise had a lot to do with wanting to be at home for your kids. When I left corporate America, it was an intentional move brought on by my desire to have children. More specifically, I wanted to have children that didn't have to spend their young years being raised by other people all day while I sat in traffic and conference rooms, missing them and wondering what abduction or bacteria might befall them at any moment.

Growing up around entrepreneurs, I guess you could say self-employment was in my blood, or at least my backyard. My husband, on the other hand, grew up with both parents working for the government. So the idea of a steady paycheck and stable benefits worked for him and, as it turns out, our household. I mean, come on, somebody has to make sure there's milk in the fridge. The steadiness of his income and the supportive nature of his soul allowed me to spread my entrepreneurial wings and fly into the home office parenthood bliss that surely awaited me.

What can I say? I was in my 20s, had never started a business before, or had a child. I had it all figured out.

Although I was a few years away from wanting to conceive, I was all too aware that home-based businesses don't often spring up overnight. I knew it would take planning and time to get prepared, hang my shingle out for the entire world (or at least the neighbors) to see, and convince everyone who would bother to listen that I was the best communications consultant going. I knew I would make plenty of mistakes, so I wanted to allow myself enough time to do that before dealing with the stresses that would inevitably accompany pregnancy and parenthood.

And I was right. It did take time, and I did make mistakes. What I wasn't prepared for was the full-time challenge of at-home parenting and an at-home business. And I learned something. Pay close attention now, because here comes the first principle behind sound home office parenting.

The secret is this: *you cannot be a full-time, hands-on parent and run a full-time, hands-on home-based business and do either one well.* Repeat this aloud. Fight it for a few minutes if you have to,

and then embrace this as a basic rule of living outside of an insti-
tution. Check your superman/woman complex at the door, and
accept this truth.

Now, you can certainly try to accomplish doing both, as I did
and as most home office parents at some point do. And I recommend you give it a spin, if only to prove to yourself the hideous
quality of life that such a pace would ensure for you and yours.
It is rife with stress, exhaustion, feelings of hopelessness and
inadequacy, and overall will render you a miserable human
being.

I'm guessing this is not exactly what you had in mind when you
set out to own your own business. This is not the kind of freedom you said you wanted, or the kind of person you had hoped
to become. You know—the one your children look to for guidance on how to live a healthy and rewarding life?

But we as fallible human beings sign up for it anyway. We tell
ourselves we can multi-task and change diapers while mentally
preparing a cutting-edge widget-selling strategy. We convince
ourselves that one more cartoon won't hurt our toddler as we
dash off that press release. When we deal with client headaches,
we assure ourselves that our four-year-old doesn't really need
the one-on-one attention we read about in parenting magazines.
After all, he gets it on weekends, right?

But here is what inevitably happens when you try to do both
full-time—something has to give. And I assure you, it will.
Because the business often pays the mortgage or creates other
financial or personal gain, however, the business is not typically what gives. It is instead, all too often, the children.

The irony here is that you wanted to work at home to be there for your children, and they are the very people who suffer from the ramifications of you trying to "do it all." There is nothing impressive or honorable about trying to have two very full-time jobs when the emotional and developmental needs of your children are slipping through the cracks.

Especially since you're a great parent. You're a fantastic business person. You're just not a superhero. You need sleep. You need sex. You need to watch a movie and eat a bag of pretzels sometimes.

And you also need to splash around in the pool with your kids. You need to go to the park and fly high on the swings next to your daughter. You need ice cream to run down your face while your son laughs at you.

You need time to reflect. Time to build shelves, put photos in albums, read a magazine and zone out in the grocery store aisles. You need time to breathe in deep and laugh out loud.

So, the first key to being a successful home office parent is recognizing the reality of the limitations on your time and energy, otherwise known as *being human*. Once you've accepted that, you need to prioritize, set boundaries that you can stick to and live with, and strategize how to get the help you need, while accomplishing the business goals you need to succeed.

Oh, is that all?

Stay with me. We'll get it done in the coming chapters.

CHAPTER ONE
Success Exercises

#1 What is/was my reason or motivation for becoming a home office parent?

#2 How does the reality of life as a home office parent differ from my expectations?

#3 What is trying to "do it all" costing me? My spouse? My children?

#4 If I weren't stretched to my limit, what would I do for enjoyment with and without my family?

#5 List three things that make you a great parent.

#6 List three things that make you a great businessperson.

CHAPTER ONE
Three Key Concepts

• The first key to being a successful home office parent is recognizing the reality of the limitations on your time and energy...otherwise known as being human.

• You cannot be a full-time, hands-on parent, and run a full-time, hands-on home-based business, and do either one well.

• What inevitably happens when you try to do both full-time? Something has to give. And because the business often pays the mortgage, what gives instead is all too often the needs of our kids.

CHAPTER ONE
Survival Strategies

- Create a *Sanity Checklist* to remind yourself why you have taken on the role of a home office parent in the first place. This will serve you well during those particularly trying moments when sliding down the wall into a human puddle feels like a logical option. Keep the checklist short, and put it where you'll see it daily. Maybe yours consists of 5 bullet points and it's on a sticky note inside the cover of your daily planner. Or, perhaps your motivators are listed on a big, laminated poster board in your office.

- **Get the scoop.** If you didn't grow up around entrepreneurs or you don't know any, go find some and talk to them. Read up online, and learn more about what this home-based business choice will likely entail before you sign up for a major life and work style change.

- **Take a test drive.** There will inevitably be an adjustment phase, so planning for it will spare you needless headaches. Take the time you require to get used to home office parenting before you fill your schedule with clients and projects. Easing in and working out your individual household kinks will help you in assessing what you can and cannot realistically pull off.

- **Beware of multitasking.** Once a time management suggestion, multitasking can and has become a lifestyle for many home office parents. And the truth is that while more mindless tasks can be accomplished this way, the overall concept often sets people up to fail. Who decided that focusing your attention on one thing was not good enough? That to be truly effective and efficient, you needed to be doing at least two things at once? In our quest to get more done in less time, we have bought into this ridiculous theory, but in practice, nothing will be completed with any level of focus, and you will likely have to backtrack to accomplish at least one of the two things you were attempting to do simultaneously, if not both.

- **Self assess.** Try to determine under what circumstances you do your best work and your best parenting. Are you more patient with your kids in the morning hours? Do you work better in the evenings, knowing everyone who can't go potty by themselves is tucked away for the night? Your schedule as a home office parent will be non-traditional at best, so determine what works for you, your family, and your business, and then plan accordingly.

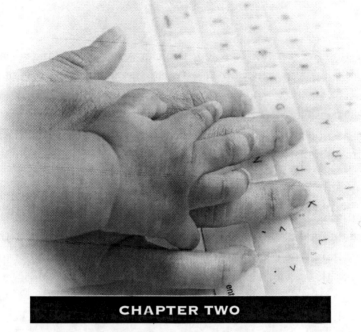

CHAPTER TWO

You May Be Ready...
But Are They?

You know a home-based business is absolutely the right choice for you. You've always wanted to be your own boss. You have considerable industry experience and a sustainable business concept. You've weighed the pros and cons, and you just know you can't lose.

And if your life were all about you, the decision would be made. But then again, if your life were all about you, you wouldn't be reading this book.

In confronting your home office readiness, it is important to confront the reality that being in business for yourself can be a *lonely* business. No water cooler chitchat, and no colleagues around the partition to whom you can vent. Networking socials and phone calls to your best friend five states away can only carry you so far, and there can and will be moments when you feel a sense of paralyzing overwhelm. These moments don't mean you're not cut out for entrepreneurship, they just mean you're human.

Now, imagine that overwhelm and, in addition to sometimes unreasonable clients and often unreliable vendors, throw parenthood in the mix. You may at first think that *lonely* is the last thing you'll feel, because you'll have the kids around and theoretically won't have a second to think about it.

The truth is that having the kids around can make you feel even more lonely. Not having an adult on-site to whom you can speak freely or with whom you can brainstorm about a client challenge, while simultaneously trying to potty train your resistant two-year old, can send the four walls closing right in on you.

Then there's your child's confusion at why Daddy is yelling at his laptop, or why, after talking to Mr. Accountant, Mommy is crying with three pens sticking out of her ponytail. You look at their little faces and you can just tell they're thinking, "I don't know why you're acting like a crazy person, but you can hold my bunny for awhile. That usually works for me."

Since Big Bird has not yet covered quarterly tax reports, and Elmo has not delved into the intricacies of computer tech complications, you can't converse with the kids about your daily entrepreneurial struggles. And, since you as a caring parent want to send positive messages to those little minds you're in charge of cultivating, you have to watch what you say and be sure to spell your expletives. If you don't, it will come back to haunt you on a play-date, in the busy express lane at the grocery store, or, as was my personal humiliation, in church.

The key to surviving this struggle is setting up a reliable network both inside and outside of your business operations. The good news is that handling this inside your business is pretty straight-forward. In selecting product manufacturers or webmasters, you interview these resources carefully, explain what you will expect from them and what they can expect from you, and set up a method of communication and a task/order fulfillment process before you begin the service agreement. You don't call them and say "We're working together" and hang up.

And so it is with the outside parties and factors that affect your home-based business. You must consider where your home team is at with this entrepreneurial notion of yours, and it's never too early to open the lines of communication about any mixed feelings, fears, assumptions or concerns that may be hovering.

You will absolutely want (and sometimes, flat out need) the support of your friends and family to get through the rough times involved in creating and sustaining your business, and hopefully you'll be able to call on the support of your spouse or partner (and your children, if they're old enough to under-stand). Talking out their feelings on this issue is just a smart and respectful way to lay a solid foundation for growth...for the business *and* the family.

Your immediate family is, of course, the most directly affected party by the choices you make and the repercussions of those choices. They have just as many assumptions about this process as you do, but your lists won't likely line up the same.

Perhaps your spouse thinks this is going to be great. He/she will get to come home to a neat and tidy abode at the day's end, with dinner prepped and ready to serve; after all, you've been "home all day." More money will be coming in, less money will be going out, stress will be eliminated and all will be right with the world.

Your kids think this is extremely fun. Mom/Dad will be home all day? Yippee! Candyland tournaments. Craft projects galore. Going to the park anytime we want!

So, give them the respect they deserve and sit down to discuss whether or not they are ready to live with and support the changes and uncertain outcomes involved with this endeavor.

You can do this without their cooperation if you have to, but it's certainly going to go much more smoothly, both professionally and personally, if your household is on your team. Their encouragement is invaluable on this journey.

And while friends and colleagues are great sources of support, keep in mind that it's easier for people who don't live with you to support you, because they're not a captive audience. They can hang up on you or leave the restaurant when you start to whine or throw things.

So, how do you determine if your family is on board with a home-based business?

STEP ONE

Make a presentation. I'm confident you can forego the Power Point slides, but present your spouse with a well-thought out explanation of why you want to work from home, how you'll accomplish this, and what short term household sacrifices may be involved in exchange for long term gains. Explain the benefits of this decision, both financial and otherwise (more free time, flexibility, low overhead, less wardrobe/commuting expenses), as well as the challenges you're sure to face.

Don't sugarcoat it. Be as honest as you can be about all aspects of this home business enterprise, because you'll need support through the rough waters. If you didn't mention there would be any rough waters at the beginning, your spouse may be more than annoyed with you when water starts flooding the home-business boat. He or she may feel lied to and betrayed, and that's a struggle you don't want to deal with when confronting a business, financial or time management problem. Be forthright from the start so there's a good chance the support will be there when you need it.

Avoid having this discussion when your mother-in-law is visiting or you're on your way out the door to the big game. Give this matter the weight it warrants, and set an appointment. For example, you can say, "Joe, I'd like to discuss the idea I mentioned to you about working from home. Can we take some time around 8pm to talk about this in the living room?"

Once you make the appointment, keep it. If you take your business seriously from the beginning, so will your family. Avoid all distractions. Make sure the kids are in bed, the phone ringer is muted, and the television is turned off. Give this discussion the attention and focus it deserves.

STEP TWO

Be clear about your needs. Surely there will be sacrifices on your part to establish and sustain your business, but your family will have to make concessions as well. Alert them to these potential conflicts from the start.

It's important to be very realistic about the time and energy you will have to put into establishing and growing your business. You may not have the energy to cook at night, or mow the lawn every Sunday. You may not have the time for social engagements you typically enjoy, or the finances for the traveling that has become part of your annual routine.

I guarantee that you will need extra understanding and support on these issues and much more. Ask for it upfront.

Also, be clear about your need for time and space. Tell your spouse if you think you'll have to work evenings and weekends for the first quarter to get things up and running. Express your need for some office space away from high-traffic areas of the house, and propose where you think that would work best. Request that when you're in your office or on the phone, that you not be disturbed. Then, indicate when your spouse can have a few hours to him/her self while you take the kids on errands.

And don't forget to ask for respect; not just that your spouse have it, but that it be demonstrated in word and deed. Just because your business is home-based does not mean it is any less professional than if you had a storefront on Main Street. If you joke that your spouse "thinks your business is a hobby," there's resentment brewing there that will inevitably damage both the marriage and the business. Confront this issue head-on if you sense (or know) it exists.

STEP THREE

Present a backup plan. Show your spouse that you have researched and planned for as many contingencies as you can conceive of, and that you have boundaries in place to avoid turning the family unit on its collective ear.

Things will go wrong and mistakes will be made, so the more planning you do and the more boundaries you have in place, the easier the process will be on everybody (more on this in Chapter 5).

And don't just have a backup plan for the struggles you're sure to face. *Plan for success.* What's the backup plan if your business takes off, you need commercial space and a staff of ten? Many home office parents plan for challenges, but few plan for success. And success has a short attention span. If you're not ready, it will find someone else who is.

STEP FOUR

Interview your family. What are their expectations? What are their fears? What are their needs? What are their boundaries? What are their priorities?

Action plan together and set up systems that work for you, your spouse, and the kids you want to enjoy before they're looking right through you at 13, cracking their gum, and saying, "Huh?"

And…little ones do get a vote. If you want them to honor your desk time, honor their park time. If you want them to zip it during a very important call, teach them hand charades. Will most of this discussion be lost on them? Sure. Is it still important that they feel like they're part of the process? You bet.

While you may be the entrepreneur, this decision affects the whole family. This interview will show the people you love the most how much you respect and value their thoughts and feelings.

STEP FIVE

Get it in writing. Outline the parameters of these negotiations so that you can point to a specific document and remind your spouse (or yourself) of the discussions had and the commitments made.

Make crayons available for young signors, and encourage an illustrative contract from your four-year old about what he thinks this will look like.

Revisit this contract every three to six months and see if the agreed upon situation is working for the family and if everyone is holding up their end of the deal. Infants are exempt, as they may eat, tear or salivate upon said contract.

CHAPTER TWO
Success Exercises

Try this home office parent contract sample, or use it as a jumping off point to create your own:

On this ___ day of _____, I,

_____,
(Spouse's Name)

being of loving, supportive mind and body, do hereby agree to support _____
(Your Name)

in his/her home-based business endeavor.

I agree to respect this unique blending of important roles in his/her life, and I promise to forgive anything said in the heat of a hard-drive crash. In return,

_____
(Your Name)

commits to the following parameters:

1. _____
2. _____
3. _____
4. _____
5. _____

_____   _____
Your Signature   Date

_____   _____
Spouse's Signature   Date

CHAPTER TWO
Three Key Concepts

- Your spouse and kids are the people most directly affected by the choices you make and the repercussions of those choices. They have just as many assumptions about this process as you do, but your lists won't likely line up the same.

- Give your family the respect they deserve and sit down to discuss whether or not they are ready to live with and support the changes and uncertain outcomes involved with this endeavor.

- The five core steps to gaining your family's support include:
  - Make a presentation.
  - Be clear about your needs.
  - Present a backup plan that factors in both struggles *and* success.
  - Interview them.
  - Get their support in writing.

CHAPTER TWO
Survival Strategies

- **Avoid "The ME Show."** We entrepreneurs can get a little self-absorbed at times about our deadlines, our commitments, our goals, and our growth. Respect that Janie's ballet recital and your spouse's work commitments need to be acknowledged and supported too.

- **Diffuse, don't confuse.** Remember that adults in an office setting can distinguish between you being upset with a client versus being just plain upset, but little ones only embrace the latter, which causes them significant confusion and sadness. Despite the fact that sometimes your kids are your only on-site staff, try to suppress the urge to vent to them about the (insert expletive here) printer, client or vendor. Instead, diffuse the stressful situation by getting the kids involved in an activity or a short video for a few minutes so you can call your spouse or a friend and quietly get the stress out of your system. Or, better yet, grab your kids and hit the park for a while. A change of scenery, some fresh air, and watching your kids run and laugh will serve all parties effectively.

- **Identify your expectations and theirs.** We all have expectations about how things will likely play out, but we don't always communicate them openly and honestly. Lead by example, and then encourage your spouse and children to share their understanding of the road ahead.

- **Quid pro quo.** Demonstrate in word and deed that you value the respect your spouse and kids have for your work time by giving quality time back to them. When you sit down to play CandyLand or read a story to your kids, give it all you've got.

Surprise your spouse by knocking out a few household chores you know said spouse does not want to come home to.

- **Remember that life happens.** You will need to renegotiate even the most balanced of schedules from time to time in order to manage growth in both the children and the business. When you're attempting to potty train your two-year old, plan for less in your work schedule that week. If you've just signed a new client with immediate needs, don't promise the kids that you'll spend the day at the pool. Smaller children will go from two naps to one nap to no naps, and older kids will want more complicated craft projects and puzzles. These changes in little developing bodies and brains will impact when you'll be able to carve out time to work, so keep in mind that things can and will shift.

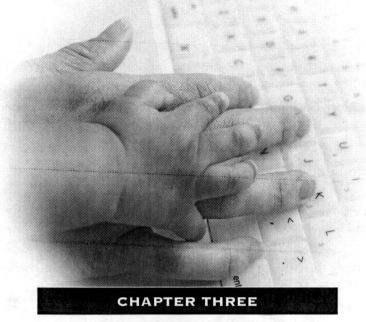

CHAPTER THREE

The Kid Factor

No one who sets out to be a home office parent plans to put their kids in front of DVDs all day or work in their pajamas until 5pm. But home office parenthood can be a slippery slope of neglect for yourself and your kids, even for the most well-intentioned mom or dad.

After all, it was those great intentions that put you here, right? "I can make more income for my family on my own, thereby setting up little Johnny for Yale tuition when he's ready," you muse. But often, you end up spending those extra tuition bucks on toys and treats, not just because you feel guilty that your kids have taken a backseat to your clients lately, but because in the back of your mind, such toys and treats will keep them busy while you get one more thing done in your office.

You say, "I can keep my little ones healthier and safer by keeping them out of day care and in our home." But it's been seven minutes since Sarah left the room to get her doll and you haven't seen or heard from her since. At the day care center—the one you dismiss as a germ warehouse—you'd be fired for not watching the children appropriately. And, at least in day care, she'd have someone who was taking the time to play dolls with her.

"I can interact with the kids so they don't just watch cartoons all day and instead have healthy outdoor time." And then the TV—which they never watched before because you knew it would corrode their young minds—gets turned on more often, as evidenced by Megan's announcement at dinner that her pasta will be on her plate for a limited time only and batteries are not included. The walks to the park become fewer and further between, and the kids are on to you about the no-longer novelty concept of having a "special day in our pajamas."

I'm well in touch with how crummy all of this feels because I have been there. You tell yourself it's not perfect, but it's the price you pay for being a business owner. In the back of your mind, however, you know who is really picking up the check.

It all hit me one day when I was talking to a colleague who was telling me how proud she was that she had the milk and the cereal on low shelves, so that her four-year old could get breakfast for herself and her three-year old sibling, thus not causing any interruption in my colleague's work schedule. The TV was set to a kid-friendly cartoon channel so the kids only had to press the "on" button for hours of entertainment. And, while sometimes she felt guilty about the situation, she told me with great pride that she "had a business to run, and if they had to watch one more DVD so she could get things done, so be it."

This mom had completely lost sight of why she started a home-based business in the first place. And while I was saddened (OK... and a little horrified) by her perception that this was not just acceptable, but was in fact something to be proud of, it forced me to take a look at my own system of checks and balances.

This colleague had come to view home office parenting as a choice: attentive parent *or* successful entrepreneur. The mentality had gone from "I want to raise my children" to an "it's 'them' or 'me'" mentality. It all probably started out as a temporary feeling stemming from a meltdown moment, but then gradually grew into a permanent mindset.

The truth is that if you respect your kids and yourself, it's not a choice. It's a synergistic lifestyle that takes lots of patience, mind-numbing (but momentary) frustration, time, trial, error, many tears (yours and theirs) and numerous hugs to figure out. There are various formulas for how it can be done well, but all of these begin with respect.

Let's start with respect for who you are and what you're capable of. To honor your role as a parent, you have to respect yourself enough to believe you deserve the job. You are an intelligent being who has been entrusted with the care of these amazing little souls. After all, your clients wouldn't give you money every month if you didn't have a skill set or two in your back pocket.

You can manage disgruntled clients, send out six proposals and pitch a reporter in a single bound, so I'm confident you can do this parenting thing. Just remember that respecting yourself as a parent means allowing yourself room to make mistakes and renegotiate along the way…without denouncing yourself as a failure to your children.

Then there's respect for your kids. Many of you started businesses because you respected your children enough to make sure they were raised the best way possible…by you. It's ironic that in our quest to provide the best for our children, they are often the very people who get pushed aside.

You also wanted the freedom and flexibility to be with your kids when you wanted to be, not when your boss said you could be. But now the only unreasonable boss that you're working for is you.

Honoring your role as a parent requires carving out time for some hands-on, fingers-in-the-paint, feet-in-the-grass parenting everyday to stay fresh and connected with these fantastic little people. When we don't make time for our kids in the name of entrepreneurship, everybody loses.

At the same time, make sure your kids have an opportunity to respect your work as something that's important to you and an endeavor which is a happy part of your life. But how do you get little ones to care about your work and what it means to you and why you do it? Lean in, here comes the secret: tell them.

My three-year old and I have great talks about what happened at pre-school that morning, and then what happened at my business meeting, which I obviously try to describe at a level she can comprehend. My six-year old has enjoyed these talks for some time now, and swears when she grows up she wants to be an "entrepren-OREO" like Mom.

The quickest way to disrespect yourself and your kids in this process is to walk around with your hands endlessly in the air, forever professing that you will never get it all done, and you were an idiot to think you could pull off life as a home office parent. By being so negatively vocal about your challenges you actually teach your kids that neither your business nor your family is a source of joy for you. You show them a person in perpetual crisis, instead of a parent in consistent balance.

We as entrepren-OREOs need to find a healthy balance between our roles in business and in life, because what is business success if it comes at a higher price than we're willing to pay? At the end of the day, being in the black means nothing if we're in the red with our kids.

CHAPTER THREE
Success Exercises

#1 Why do/did I want to have a home-based business?

#2 What does my business mean to me? Why do I do it?

#3 How do I define a "good parent?"

#4 How do I define a "successful entrepreneur?" What does success look like to me as an individual?

#5 Five things my kids and I love to do together are:

#6 Five things I want to tell my children about my business are:

CHAPTER THREE
Three Key Concepts

- Teach your kids that your intentions line up with your actions. If you want to stay at home to give your kids the attention and focus they deserve, engage them without your laptop in front of you. If you say that you're at home to connect with them during these early formative years, learn how to shut the office door and open up a dialogue.

- Avoid walking around with your hands endlessly in the air, forever professing that you will never get it all done, and you were an idiot to think you could pull off life as a home office parent. By being so negatively vocal about your challenges, you teach your kids that neither your business nor your family is a source of joy for you. You show them a person in perpetual crisis, instead of a parent in consistent balance.

- Make sure your kids have an opportunity to respect your work as something that's important to you and an endeavor which is a happy part of your life. Tell them all about what your work means to you and why you do it.

CHAPTER THREE
Survival Strategies

- **Predict unpredictability.** Remember that life with little ones is notoriously unpredictable, so keep that in mind when making plans. If there is a business appointment or event that you simply cannot miss, have a plan should your babysitter bail on you.

- **Plan for the wiggle room you'll need.** If you have a conference call at 1pm, don't put the baby down for a nap at 12:58pm. She will let you (and your fellow callers) know just how not tired she is at precisely the wrong moment. Get to know the delicate ratio of what you think your kids will do with what can actually go horribly awry, and pad your schedule accordingly.

- **Understand that little bodies get big sick germs.** Immunity is something that kids are building up right now, which can flat out knock down all of your meetings, projects and must-do's of the day. I promise you that your three-year old will have double ear infections and a 103° fever the night you're on a significant deadline, so accept early on that colds and flu's will get in the way sometimes.

- **Have a contingency plan.** In the event of one of these ill-timed illnesses, have a backup plan. In my work, I am very upfront about the fact that I am a mother first. I make no apologies for this, so my clients understand they'll get the best I have to give to their projects, but not in the name of withholding the best I have to give to my children. Because I am clear about this from the beginning, any unforeseen child challenges are not catastrophic.

- **Plan for a *Spouse-On-Call* arrangement.** At our house, for the most part, I'm the one who gets up with the kids if something goes bump in the night, and I'm the one who holds them through the tummy aches and overall ouches...unless I'm on a significant deadline that I can't extend. Then it's understood that my spouse takes over, his needed appearance at his office the next day notwithstanding. I don't invoke this arrangement often, so when it's needed, he doesn't question its necessity. This is one of those situations where supporting your business in word is easier than doing so in deed.

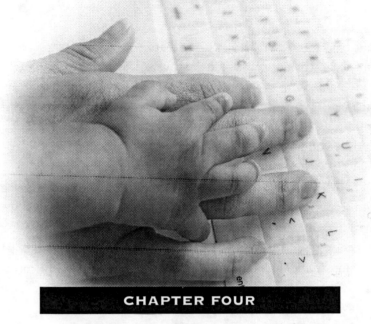

CHAPTER FOUR

In Business & In Balance

Achieving balance as a home office parent requires looking at what your success goals are, how you manage your time, what roles you play and the priorities to which you're committed. I know this exceptionally well because I started out doing none of these things.

Having started my business before conceiving my first child, I had a steady but small group of clients by the time my daughter, Diane, was born. I hired a mother's helper to support me with the baby's care, so that I would have some time to work and continue to grow the business. And grow it did.

As Diane took incredible steps, so too did my business. Fast forward two years to a beautiful, spacious house on the river near Aspen, a nice car, a full-time nanny, a personal chef, a country club membership and a house-cleaning service. My hard work had paid off, right? Getting up at 5am to get right in my office and start working, and then faxing out materials at midnight had enabled me to achieve significant and rapid growth in my business. My business was in fourteen major cities and four countries, I had lots of staff and stuff, a happy marriage and a healthy baby. I had achieved Success with a capital S.

Or had I? We rarely entertained in that beautiful, spacious house on the river because I was always working. I didn't get to drive that nice car very often because I was always working. I'm sure the country club pool was fun for the nanny and Diane, but I was inside the club's restaurant or office space in client meetings.

My happy marriage was more of an assumption than a reality because I wasn't paying enough attention to know the difference (luckily I assumed correctly). And having a wonderful, albeit ever-present, nanny rush into your office to tell you, "Come quick…she's about to take her first step" has at once a joyful and incredibly depressing ring to it.

I had set out to become a home office parent, but I turned around one day to find that someone else was doing the parenting. My being on site made no difference in my daughter's life whatsoever, because I was hardly ever in her line of sight.

And that was it for me. In one fell swoop it became clear to me that I had signed up for someone else's definition of success. I didn't know what my definition was yet, I just knew it wasn't this. So, I did the unthinkable. I gave success away.

After letting the nanny go and cutting back on my workload, I did not experience the relief and sense of peace that I expected, at first. I felt fear and self-doubt and, well, pretty much like I was a complete idiot for walking away from a lifestyle at twenty-nine that many people spend their entire lives trying to achieve.

I was really beginning to question my choice. One day, as if sensing my need for affirmation, Diane walked into my bedroom, looked at me, and said, "No more nannies, Mommy. Just Mommy and Diane."

And then I felt it. The relief. The sense of peace. The knowledge that if I built it once, I could build it again…later. For now, my daughter felt valued and honored and seen and heard by my choice—by her mother. So, as it turned out, my success definition had less to do with stuff and more to do with life… and that was just fine by me.

Before you can live in balance, which is essential to happy home office parenting, you have to understand what definition of success you're trying to attain and where you're putting your energy, because the two may not line up. Let's find out.

Step One: Success Defined

In Chapter Three's *Success Exercises*, I asked you to begin to cultivate your definition of success, because you have to know what you're trying to achieve if you'll ever know whether or not you've achieved it. Pursuing "success" and "balance" are fruitless endeavors because those are ethereal, vague concepts that are just floating out there in the air, not rooted in specific behaviors or defined by any measure.

Before you can complete *The Balance Sheet* exercises at the end of this chapter, you'll need some clarity on your individual perceptions and definitions of how you want to work and live.

After referring back to the *Success Exercises* in Chapter Three, think more specifically about what success looks like to you, and complete this sentence:

My definition of success is:

Now that you can describe your individual definition of success, describe what living a life in balance might look like by completing this sentence:

My definition of balance is:

Step Two: Priorities Assessed

After you've created your definitions of success and balance, turn your attention toward your priorities. What are they? Maybe they include spending a certain amount of time each day focused on your kids, or achieving a specific annual income, or healthy living through regular fitness and nutrition.

What matters most to you? Assess at least five priorities in your life.

My top five priorities are:
  1.
  2.
  3.
  4.
  5.

Step Three: Roles Identified

Armed with this knowledge, look at where your time typically goes. Begin by defining the top five characters you play on the stage that is your life. I am, for example, a busy actress playing the roles of:

Self
Wife
Mother
Business Owner
Friend

Everything I do falls under one of those headings. If I spend time volunteering, that falls under "Friend." If I play fetch with our dog Mitch, that falls under "Mother." If I read a book for my book club, that falls under "Self."

Although we don't necessarily recall auditioning for the parts, we all play a cast of characters to over-eager audiences everyday. These roles can be difficult to sort out, much less manage. If, for example, you are a musician by trade, that falls under "Business Owner," but if you play for fun, that falls under "Self." If you volunteer your business as an event sponsor, that falls under "Business Owner," but if you volunteer your time to deliver food to those in need, that might fall under "Friend."

To balance your time effectively and attain the success you seek, you must first identify the parts you play.

My top five roles are:
    1.
    2.
    3.
    4.
    5.

Step Four: Time Confronted

Have you ever caught yourself saying "I'll find the time" or "I'll make the time?", as if extra time is just hiding under a rock somewhere waiting for you?

The truth is that if you get the eight hours of sleep you're supposed to get for healthy living, that only leaves 16 hours a day for you to live out all five of your roles. So, if you're trying to cram 24 hours of role playing into 16 hours per day, it's no wonder that your whole life feels like a fifty-yard dash.

Examine where your time is going by charting it on *The Imbalance Sheet* at the end of this chapter. Does your time spent line up with your priorities and definition of success? Or is your daily living inconsistent with what matters to you?

Next, complete *The Balance Sheet* exercise. This time, complete it as it would appear if your daily living were consistent with your goals and values. Then, tape a copy to anything that will stand still so you'll have a snapshot of your desired life in front of you.

CHAPTER FOUR
Success Exercises

The Imbalance Sheet

AM/PM	Sunday	Monday	Tuesday	Wednesday
6:00 AM				
7:00 AM				
8:00 AM				
9:00 AM				
10:00 AM				
11:00 AM				
12:00 PM				
1:00 PM				
2:00 PM				
3:00 PM				
4:00 PM				
5:00 PM				
6:00 PM				
7:00 PM				
8:00 PM				
9:00 PM				

The Balance Sheet

AM/PM	Sunday	Monday	Tuesday	Wednesday
6:00 AM				
7:00 AM				
8:00 AM				
9:00 AM				
10:00 AM				
11:00 AM				
12:00 PM				
1:00 PM				
2:00 PM				
3:00 PM				
4:00 PM				
5:00 PM				
6:00 PM				
7:00 PM				
8:00 PM				
9:00 PM				

CHAPTER FOUR
Three Key Concepts

- Before you can live in balance, which is essential to happy home office parenting, you have to understand what definition of success you're trying to attain and where you're putting your energy, because the two may not line up.

- Achieving balance as a home office parent requires looking at what your success goals are, how you manage your time, what roles you play and the priorities to which you're committed.

- Confront how you spend your time. If you're trying to cram 24 hours of role playing into 16 hours per day, it's no wonder that your whole life feels like a fifty-yard dash.

CHAPTER FOUR
Survival Strategies

- **Don't let the business run you.** You're the entrepreneur, so remember that you run the business. If there's imbalance in play, you have the power to grab hold of the reigns and renegotiate.

- **When is enough enough?** Figure out what your ideal work and lifestyle look like before the business takes off, so you don't lose sight of the goal in your mad pursuit to succeed.

- **Match up wants and needs.** How many hours of your time does your business need to achieve the level of success you seek? How many hours can you, or are you willing to, realistically give it? Does the math work?

- **Get rid of roles that don't serve you.** If you play the role of "Put-Upon Martyr," give it up. If you play the role of "Slave to Your Clients," give it up. These roles chip away at who you are and build resentment toward your business and your life.

- **Sleep.** People who have been to medical school and who have studied the affects of limited sleep over long periods of time all say the same thing: get your eight hours. Do not convince yourself that you can go without sleep. It will ultimately cause big problems in your mental and physical health, which will cause big problems in your attempt to be a lucid home office parent.

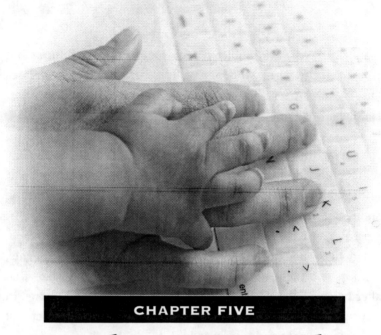

CHAPTER FIVE

Boundaries You Need to Set & Stick To

There is one common denominator among all successful home office parents: they know that a business without boundaries is a business that fails.

Boundaries have gotten a bad rap in recent years as things you have to put in place to block something out. Instead, think of boundaries as something you use to protect what's within. While your business is a big part of your life, identifying and establishing boundaries that work for you—before you need them—will help you to avoid letting your business take over your life.

"Bah," you say. "I would never let that happen." Unfortunately, that's what every home office parent thinks in the beginning. But before you know it, blurring the lines has ultimately compromised your success in both business and life, led to resentment, and even burnout.

Have you met my friend, Burnout? He and I are intimately acquainted. Did I take a step back to focus on the parenting part of the home office parent equation? You bet. And then I took another step *way* back.

I had been on the phone with colleagues, prospects, clients, vendors and the media all day, every day, for so many years that after I *slowed down*, I found myself avoiding a ringing phone. In fact, I grew to hate talking on the phone for the simple fact that I was completely and utterly sick of it.

I had written so many press releases, articles, brochures, web sites and newsletters that once I *slowed down*, the thought of writing a few paragraphs threw me into a tailspin. I didn't just have writer's block; I had a full-blown writer's fortress between me and the keyboard.

"Slowing down," as I refer to it, sounds nice and easy, doesn't it? What we're really talking about here is burnout. Simultaneous to my burnout came a diabetes diagnosis, and I realized I needed to fully retreat in order to heal from the last few years of being relentless in my business endeavors.

Another hard-charging entrepreneur and dear friend has endured burnout more than once during his thirty years on the course. He describes it like this:

"You're going, and you're going and you're going. You can't

stop because it would be like jumping out of a moving car on the freeway. You've created too much momentum in your business to stop even for a moment. Your clients are counting on you. Your family is counting on the lifestyle you've created for them. First Federal is counting on your hefty mortgage payment. The kids are counting on ballet lessons and family vacations. Your church is counting on your weekly contribution. That Mercedes won't pay for itself.

And then...kaboom. You do stop. And stop short, with rubber-laden skid marks behind you. And you feel as though you could just sit in a chair for six months and eat cereal out of a box. You are completely depleted, with the added bonus of knowing you failed your business, yourself and your family.

And then, once healed, you slide back through the window of the racecar only to accelerate again, swearing you won't go too fast this time."

If you haven't been there, you obviously don't want to go there. And here's the good news: you don't have to, because boundaries that you set up *and stick to* prevent the imbalance that leads to burnout.

Once healed, I decided I cared about myself and my family too much to let that happen again. I kept my hand in the business world with the occasional published article, speaking engagement, or pro bono client, but I stayed focused on balance, my family, my health and our second daughter, Megan, with whom we were blessed. Every few months or so I'd take on a little more—a monthly column this quarter, a new consulting client that quarter.

I took a hard look at what working without boundaries had cost me and then set up systems to prevent that from reoccurring. Now a profitable, balanced and boundary-loving home office parent, I have some boundary suggestions for you to achieve your own balanced and burnout-free life.

Be the Enforcer.

This whole process starts with a solid commitment. There is no point in setting up boundaries that you're unwilling to enforce. Effective balance is achieved when you're committed to the process, even if you have to put a client on a waiting list or say no to box seats at the big game. Being the boundary enforcer is rarely fun because you're inevitably disappointing someone. This is particularly difficult to do when it's a client who wants to pay you money, or it's a close friend or family member who pouts and fusses at you to change your mind—and I'm not talking about the kids here.

Be honest with yourself.

Look at *The Balance Sheet* exercise from Chapter 4. Remember your definition of success, your priorities, your roles, and the fact that you only have 16 hours a day to make it all happen and—dare I say it?—enjoy it. Set up boundaries that honor what you say you want.

It's important to note here that these have to be boundaries that work for you, not boundaries that work for your best friend or your favorite colleague. I remember my friend telling me that upon having a new baby, the advice she received from numerous women was to let the housework go, forget about the dishes, and let the dust fall where it will. One problem: my friend could not relax and bond with baby in a completely disorganized environment, so that was not advice that worked for her. In fact, it had the opposite effect and stressed her out even more. She instead chose to give up an hour of sleep to make sure things were in order, as that made managing baby's needs easier and allowed truly relaxed, quality time.

So, what do you want, and when? How does your definition of success break down into increments of time? Funnel it down logically:

Successful Life

↓

5 Year Goals

↓

1 Year Goals

↓

90 Day Goals

↓

30 Day Goals

↓

Weekly Action Plans

Look at the details of what you're trying to achieve and how they fit in with your available time. Ask yourself specific questions and answer them honestly. For example, how many hours per week do you want to bill? Then add at least ten hours per week to that figure so that you have time allocated for office administration, marketing, networking and other non-billable activities. Set the boundary that once you hit that hourly mark, you'll confront management options like outsourcing, or you'll offer to put new clients or opportunities on a waiting list.

Who is your ideal client?

Entrepreneurs often take on less-than-ideal clients for a variety of reasons, not the least of which is the uncertainty of when or if another client will ever come knocking. Such clients drag down your spirit, time and finances, and often ending up costing you more than you are ever paid.

Make a list of what your dream client looks like. How does he act? What qualities does she possess? Attracting your preferred clients first involves identifying who they are and what kind of business you really want.

Be on guard and try to spot red-flag prospects before you contract with them. While new clients are interviewing you, be sure to interview them right back. Why are they no longer working with the last service provider? What did the previous product lack that they're hoping yours will provide?

Do they expect services outside of normal business hours? Most home office parents are not able to provide customer support immediately or around the clock, so be clear about your availability from the beginning. Outline the scope of work or product functions carefully, and be specific about what you don't do or the product is not designed to do, in order to avoid any inappropriate expectations down the road. Finally, consider a thirty-day trial period for both parties to ensure that your working relationship is a good fit.

Honoring your role as a parent means avoiding difficult clients who prevent you from being able to enjoy your family time because you're too wound up and stressed out to relax or enjoy your spouse, your kids or yourself. In many cases, high-maintenance clients can even preclude you from even getting a good night's sleep, which renders you less than patient with your kids and less than your business best the next day.

The truth is that sometimes you have to say no to business in order to say yes to success.

Differentiate between work and life.

Shut the office door, turn off the Blackberry, and forget about the cell phone. At a certain point each day, you need to be able to turn off work and turn on life. If you don't, your business may skyrocket…at the expense of your health, time with your kids, relationships with family and friends, and the freedom you said you wanted when you launched your business.

Establish boundaries with your kids and your spouse. Work time is work time and family time is family time. When Mom is in the office, the kids go to Dad or Aunt Jane with snack requests and potty dilemmas. When Dad is on a call with a client, Mom doesn't force him to have a silent conversation with hand charades regarding where he put little Jimmy's sneakers.

The key here is to lead by example. If you say you'll shut the office door at 5pm, do it. Your spouse and kids will be more apt to respect the boundaries if you do, too.

You run your business…your clients don't.

Set a fair price and stick to it. Figure out policies and procedures that work best for you and your type of business, and don't change them to suit your clients. Even if your client begs you to, don't agree to take on additional services you don't really know how to provide in an effort to appear "comprehensive" in your approach; give them a few qualified leads you've identified through networking instead.

Different rules for different clients can set up a juggling act that's difficult to sustain, and ever-changing practices and fees send a message to your prospects that you lack confidence and certainty about your own business…so why would they hand you theirs?

Just say no.

If you have a great marketing opportunity, but it's at the expense of having to miss a major family milestone, it may not be worth it. If a friend needs your help, but you'll miss a deadline (and possibly lose a client) to do it, you may have to help your friend tomorrow. You can do it all, just not all at the same time.

If you're not sure whether you can say yes or no, don't jump to yes. Offer to check your schedule and get back to the inquiring party. That will give you the time to weigh the opportunity more carefully.

Draft a few key phrases to keep in your back pocket for when you need to decline a new prospect or a friend's request. "Sorry, Jim, but I'm on deadline for a major client. How about next Saturday?" or "Thanks for the opportunity to work together, Patty, but I can't take on any more clients at this time without compromising my service."

What have you done for you lately?

I remember reading that during a recession, the first thing companies typically cut is the marketing budget, which is a huge business mistake. Since most companies do this, you have a real opportunity to garner business by speaking your message louder than ever during a recession.

Similarly, in our quest to manage kids and business effectively, the first thing home office parents cut out is self-care. When we don't take time to replenish our energy, relax and re-charge, we're so depleted that we can't give anything to anybody else.

Think about the oxygen masks on an airplane. The flight attendant is quick to remind you to affix your mask first and then those of your children. Why not meet your kids' needs first? Because if you pass out, you're of no use to anyone, least of all your kids.

Not taking care of yourself leads to problems in other arenas as well. The quality of your work suffers. The time with your kids is less than quality. Fitness and nutrition fly out the window, and then you're left to deal with health problems. Opportunities are missed that you're too harried or exhausted to pursue. Financial costs add up in the form of missed tax deductions or late fees because of the pace you've adopted.

Get yourself a planner and block out regular time off from being a business owner and a parent. Call it something official in case you have a client in front of you. I call it *Staff Meeting*…party of one.

Additionally, take regular vacation time, even if you don't go anywhere. Plan for maternity or paternity leave when a new baby is on the way. Claim the time you need to be a human being.

Establishing boundaries and executing them with tact and professionalism doesn't make you selfish or unmotivated; rather, it makes you a dedicated business owner *and* human being whose work *and* life *and* kids have value.

Instead of throwing your hands in the air in the name of overwhelm, put them back on the wheel and steer your course.

CHAPTER FIVE
Success Exercises

#1 How over extended and burnout friendly am I right now?

#2 What are some boundaries from this chapter that I can put in place right now?

#3 What are three 30-day goals that I have right now? What weekly actions can I take to achieve those goals in the next month?

Goal A:
> Week One Action
> Week Two Action
> Week Three Action
> Week Four Action

Goal B:
> Week One Action
> Week Two Action
> Week Three Action
> Week Four Action

Goal C:
> Week One Action
> Week Two Action
> Week Three Action
> Week Four Action

#4 Who is my ideal client?

#5 What is one key phrase I can use to "just say no?"

#6 What are five things I enjoy doing to take care of myself?

CHAPTER FIVE
Three Key Concepts

- While your business is a big part of your life, identifying and establishing boundaries that work for you—before you need them—will help you to avoid letting your business take over your life.

- Boundaries that you set up and stick to prevent the imbalance that leads to burnout.

- Sometimes you have to say no to business in order to say yes to success.

CHAPTER FIVE
Survival Strategies

• **Start a** *This Is Why* **file,** otherwise known as a *Get Happy* file
for those times when you feel burnout lurking and you can't
remember why you ever willingly signed up for this ridiculous
life assignment. When a client sends you a thank you email
about how you really nailed their project, print it out and put
it in the file. When you get a compliment from a member of
an audience you just spoke to, write it down and put it in the
file. When you receive news coverage (that you're happy
about), put it in the file. And when another parent has a child
challenge, and asks you how you would handle it, put it in the
file. Then, when life hits you hard, grab the file and your
cocktail of choice, and have a good reminder about why you
do what you do.

• **Create a** *Burnout Buster* **action plan.** If you're too far gone
for the *Get Happy* file, schedule a "conference" or "staff semi-
nar" where you create the space to recharge and recoup by
taking some time off…even if it's one day. Give permission to
one close friend or colleague to act as a human yield sign and
let you know when you're running too hard. Take steps to get
your strength, energy and motivation back.

• **Take the time to create a comprehensive client intake
package.** The more questions you ask upfront, the fewer sur-
prises you'll have later, and the more boundaries you can put
in place to create harmonious working relationships. I have
only had one dissatisfied client in more than ten years of
business, and he was the only client I allowed to forego my
27-page intake package. Hmm…

- **Shut down your life before you boot up your work.** Don't skip off to your office in the middle of the bedtime routine or get on the phone during the dinnertime prayer. Be present in your life, do what needs to be done, and then move on to your office with the clarity and space you need to work effectively.

- **Practice saying NO.** Even if you could probably pull it off, try saying no to things that you don't want to do. In saying yes to everyone and everything, you eventually say no to healthy home office parenthood.

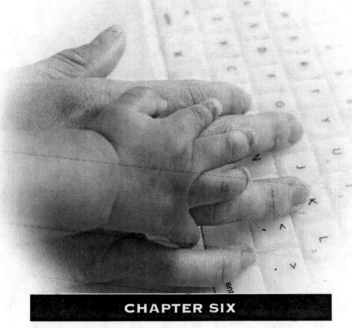

CHAPTER SIX

Get the Help You Need

Remember at the beginning of the book when I revealed the truth about home office parenting? The idea that *you cannot be a full-time, hands-on parent and run a full-time, hands-on home-based business, and do either one well*, is one of the toughest to accept. So, if the concept makes you bristle, you're not alone.

We are a society that dismisses "I can't" as the chant of the weak and the lazy, so we don't want to hear about what we cannot do. But the key component to the whole idea is the last part: *and do either one well.*

You are physically able to do both, but if you're reading this, I am confident that you don't want to be the parent that relies on DVDs everyday or the parent who burns out because the pace has finally broken you. To truly honor both roles, sometimes you have to call in reinforcements.

I did just that by hiring a mother's helper…initially. That would have been fine, had I not grown the business so rapidly. Ending up with a full-time nanny was not in the original plan, but who was I to argue with explosive growth?

As it turns out, I was just the person. After adopting a much more reasonable pace, I went to the other side of the spectrum and found it difficult to ask for help. I was gun shy about hiring someone again, even part-time, and I didn't want to bother my friends and family. But because I derive great joy from both my kids and my work, I eventually got over it.

Getting Over It

You may have a tough time asking for help, but I encourage you too to get over it. You can either ask for help or you can beat yourself up daily that you're half a business owner and half a parent, and write yourself off as some incapable mess who can't do anything 100%. Choose the former, because how you treat yourself is a living directive to your kids about the self-respect, or lack thereof, you want them to have.

What Kind of Help?

Before you can ask for help, first figure out what kind of help is most critical to your functional business. Are things more hectic in the mornings, afternoons or evenings? Can you designate all business meetings to one or two days per week? Depending on your kids' ages, why not schedule your office administration for when they're around, and give them an important sticker job while you file?

It's Not a Nanny or Nothing

There is absolutely nothing wrong with having full-time help if that is what works for you. Many of my colleagues have full-time nannies, and with this level of help comes the freedom to slam the office door shut at 5pm and roll around with your kids, because you know you had plenty of work time available to you that day. Your weekends are then full of quality family time and are truly your own—to picnic in the park, drive to the beach, or spend the day at the museums when other home office parents may be trying to squeeze in work time because the other spouse is on-site. If this is what your work style or type of business dictates, and it's how you show up best for your kids, make no apologies for it.

But for the many home office parents who want a more hands-on role with the kids during the day, or for whom full-time help is cost-prohibitive, getting some help does not necessarily mean that you have to hire a full-time nanny. Maybe your spouse can leave work early two nights a week on days where you need more help, and then he/she can work later on two other nights to make up the time while you manage the kids.

Perhaps you can look into a nanny-share program through a local agency or a mom in your playgroup, or maybe Grandma can take the kids one day a week. Is there a somewhat responsible neighborhood teenager looking for extra cash who can walk to your house? If teen judgment scares you, remember that you will be on-site. Or how about hiring an elementary education major from the local college? Expand your thinking and get creative; there are resources all around you.

Other Home Office Parents

What about joining forces with other home office parents? Perhaps you and the home office parent down the block can help each other out with scheduling. You take his kids in the morning and he takes yours in the afternoon. Then you each get at least a few quality hours of work in that day. You can find these home office parents at local networking groups and maybe just by asking the members of your book club or the guys in your softball league.

Look around for home office parents who are pulling it off, and ask them to share their strategies with you. One of my clients has a nanny who comes in three days a week, so she schedules all of her off-site meetings on those three days only. She has no expectation of accomplishing work on the other four days of the week when her kids are awake, so she gets emails returned and paperwork accomplished when they nap or go to bed. She guards her time carefully and has learned not to over-commit and overextend herself.

Your Kids Want You to Get the Help

No, you say. My kids want me! Sure they do—when you're not stressed out and when you can be fully present with them. Ever catch yourself and realize that your three-year old has been talking to you for about five minutes, but you haven't heard a word she's said? Because even though your body was at the ice cream shop, your mind was on that direct mail piece that needed to go out; the new accountant you needed to find; and whether that web site programmer would ever be finished.

If it's one thing my kids continually teach me, it is that they are consistently more observant than I realize. Having someone else who can be present with them and who is invested in creating and playing with them is far more exciting to them than to have me and my laptop in the room while they entertain themselves and I check my email. In those moments, they know my mind is not with them, and they are not my focus. That's not the message we want to send little people whose minds and attitudes we're shaping with everything we say and do.

Get the help you need for those times that you absolutely must work, so that your kids are being stimulated and shown that they are valued. Then, after you get some quality work time in, you'll have the opportunity to scoop them up, fully focused, and value the heck out of them.

Selecting a Caregiver

When figuring out the best course for your family, remember that your kids do better when the caregiver chosen to help is consistent. Having various babysitters rotating in and out of the house can be unsettling at best to little ones, and different sets of rules and behavior expectations from various adults can be downright confusing and frustrating.

Parenting experts and studies teach us that kids thrive when they know what's coming next, so factor stability and a reasonable period of longevity into your caregiver choice. Don't be afraid to discuss the stability you want to impart so they know that you'd like to set up a consistent relationship, versus grabbing some help on the fly.

Ask possible caregiver candidates about their background as it relates to caring for and relating to children. Ask them what challenges came up when sitting for other children and how they resolved them. Try things out on a trial basis before committing to a long-term agreement. See if there's a good fit, because even the most qualified caregiver may simply not have chemistry with your kids.

Look on nanny agency web sites or pick up a book on selecting a caregiver to find a comprehensive interviewing procedure. My concern for purposes of this book is more about you making the choice to get the help you need. When bringing in a stranger, you only need to watch the nightly news to know how important references, background checks and comprehensive interviews are for your children's safety.

The Caregiver's Perspective

While your caregiver obviously works for you, there are behaviors you can exhibit that will set the whole situation up to succeed or fail. A few tips for keeping caregivers happy include:

- Show respect for the caregiver, both to him/her directly, as well as in how you speak about him/her when he/she is not around. You want the caregiver to feel appreciated, but you also want your kids to understand that you trust and value this person.

- Explain to your kids that the caregiver is in charge when he/she is there, and they must respect and follow the rules as if they were coming out of your mouth.

- Emphasize that even though you are on-site, the kids are to go to the caregiver with questions or needs…not to your office.

- Honor that the caregiver may do things slightly different than you do. While you don't want to support a radical change in rules, try not to contradict him/her, especially in front of the children.

  If the caregiver says they can have a small dessert after lunch, don't jump in front of him/her and make giant sundaes for everyone. If the caregiver says it's time to settle down and read some books, don't make a face and say, "Oh, just let them run around and be kids." If you have an issue with how he/she handles something, bring it up later, out of the kids' earshot.

- Compliment and show your appreciation for the caregiver regularly, and surprise him/her with a small gift card or other token of thanks. Remember that dealing with little ones all day can exhaust even the saintliest of caregivers' patience and energy.

CHAPTER SIX
Success Exercises

#1 What gets in my way at the idea of asking for help?

#2 What kind of help do I need?

#3 Who are three people I can ask or what are three ways I can get the help I need?

#4 What steps will I take to create a positive foundation for a caregiver to come in?

CHAPTER SIX
Three Key Concepts

- You can either ask for help or you can beat yourself up daily that you're half a business owner and half a parent, and write yourself off as some incapable mess who can't do anything 100%. Choose the former, because how you treat yourself is a living directive to your kids about the self-respect, or lack thereof, you want them to have.

- Expand your thinking and get creative; there are resources all around you.

- Having someone else who can be present with your kids and who is invested in creating and playing with them is far more exciting to them than to have you and your laptop in the room while they entertain themselves and you check your email.

CHAPTER SIX
Survival Strategies

- **What help works for you?** Consider everything from day care solutions to pre-school programs to full time nannies to taking turns with other home office parents. Evaluate your options and the needs of your business, and choose what works for you (not your mother).

- **Set parameters ahead of time.** Decide early on if you'll be willing to expand your child care support solutions in relation to how big your business grows, or if there's a limit to how much help you're willing to recruit in the name of entrepreneurship. If full-time support is a deal-breaker for your work-life vision, then you'll have to limit the growth of your business. If you're unwilling to travel overnight for business, know that upfront.

- **Mind your business.** If you have interviewed, background-checked, observed and ultimately chosen your child care support resource, trust it enough to get some work done. If something is amiss, you'll pick up on it during the quality time you'll have with your children after you've had the time and space to finish your work.

- **Give care back to the care giver.** If a friend or family member is your helper of choice, be sure to reciprocate by giving them equal time back to get some things done. If you don't, resentment will build up and offers of help may be quietly withdrawn.

- **Now, get the other help you need.** Once you've achieved trusted care for the children, what support do you need within your business or within the home to help all facets of the home office parenting equation to compute?

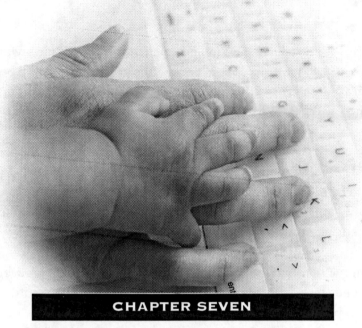

CHAPTER SEVEN

The Spousal Perspective

Much like you are managing two careers as both an entrepreneur and a parent, your spouse or partner who works outside the home and keeps those health benefits rolling in ends up having two careers as well—that he/she didn't necessarily sign up for.

Aside from your own challenges and opportunities as a home office parent, you need to remember that your spouse is directly affected by the choices you make. If you take on a new client that you don't necessarily have the time for, then that work will inevitably cut into the time you would have otherwise spent managing the household or the kids. Or, if you get backed up on filing and organization, you may have to spend Friday night straightening it all out...instead of going to dinner with your spouse.

Many is the day my husband has come home to hear me saying, "Please call for Chinese food and get the girls bathed and to bed because I had something come up" as I zip past him and duck into the office. Well, I did say *please*.

Of course, this is after asking him to swing by the dry cleaners unless he wants to wear our drapes to the office the next day; and by the way, we're out of milk and diapers, so a grocery store drive-by is a must on the way home; and boy, I sure could go for a latte after this long day I've had.

On the black-and-white TV set playing in his head, it probably sounds more like, "Here's a cocktail darling. How was your day? The pot roast is just about finished." I doubt this lunacy we sometimes call our lives is what he had in mind when he promised to love, honor and cherish, because, let's face it, the home office parent is sometimes difficult to cherish.

But cherish me he does, albeit sometimes through clenched teeth, because ultimately he supports me as a professional and a parent, respects my work, and above all knows that no one can raise our girls better than we can.

As mentioned in Chapter Two, the spousal readiness factor is a big one when it comes to diving into home office parenthood. As much as you need to take steps to value your children through this process, your spouse needs some respect too. A few ways to pull that off include:

Start Talking, Keep Talking

You and your spouse can't have enough discussion about this

adventure before it begins. Regular check-ins, once the bar has come down and you're locked into the ride (with your kids at the controls), are essential. Things grow and change, namely your kids and your business, so open communication about that growth and those changes has to happen in order to maintain connection.

You're In It Together

While this may technically be your business, everything about it affects your spouse, from the income and expenses, to the scheduling headaches and crusty dishes. Honor your spouse's role by running business obstacles and opportunities by him to get his input. Ask for her opinion before making a key decision. Remind him of how much you value his feedback. Call her and share a client victory. Involve your spouse as more than household and childcare support in your business if you want him/her to be invested in supporting it and you.

Everything You Don't Get To

Remember that everything "you don't get to" lands in your spouse's lap. If you're on a deadline and the kitchen is a biohazard, who has to clean it up upon returning from the office? If you haven't gotten around to defrosting the chicken or packing pre-school lunches, whom does that fall on?

While these things will happen from time to time, it's important to acknowledge your spouse as more than the cleanup brigade, and express your appreciation for his/her support. Try to work in some time every morning and every afternoon to do your share around the house so your spouse doesn't feel over-whelmed.

Get creative and involve the kids. My girls have great fun with Laundry Basketball, where we put a large laundry basket in the center of the bedroom hallway and everybody throws their clothes from their individual hamper into the hallway basket. Points and prizes are awarded.

Or teach your four-year old some math skills and allot different coin rewards for different doable chores. "All dollies in the toy chest" gets you a shiny quarter, and "putting the board game pieces back in the box" goes for 10 cents. Incorporate coin recognition and then add up their earnings.

It's Not A Contest

Ever hear yourself telling your spouse:

"At least you get eight hours of uninterrupted work you can count on everyday."

"When you're driving to and from work, you have time to your-self just to think…and you don't have to listen to Elmo's Greatest Hits."

"You get to talk to grownups all day and go out to lunch."

Ever hear your spouse tell you:

"Well, I have to leave the house before you're even out of bed."

"At least you can squeeze in some downtime and shopping or a couple hours at the pool."

"What did you do all day anyway?"

Here's the thing. You (ideally) made this choice together. There is no prize awarded for *He Who Suffers Most*. There are plenty of people and forces outside your front door that will take steps to knock you down, so try not to beat each other up emotionally. While occasional arguments will arise, try to prevent them from becoming habitual.

If there are repetitive situations that are not working, put your heads together and problem solve. After all, you run your own business. You raise great kids. You can work out the little things.

Be a Non-Home Office Parent

Step out of your daily roles and just be a partner sometimes. Forget the pressures of raising kids and raising profits. Go out to dinner. Drink coffee and read the paper together on the couch. Dance around the living room. Celebrate your relationship and it will cushion the daily grind from eroding your communication.

The 6pm Data Dump

At 6pm, perhaps your spouse is the first adult you've seen today. Don't punish him/her for it by talking incessantly about your day, complaining about the printer jam... and the raspberry jam on the printer... and how you didn't even get a shower until 3pm.

Let your spouse in the door…maybe even let her get her coat off first, before you start in with a rant about your day. Be sure to share the positive aspects of what happened; the fact that your direct mail campaign is getting a great response or that little Anna drew all of her shapes today. Be sure to ask about your spouse's day as well.

As much as you respect your spouse's perspective and input, you will be respected. As much as you support your spouse's challenges, you will be supported. As with anything in marriage, it's a two-way street.

CHAPTER SEVEN
Success Exercises

#1 Do I feel my spouse respects my role as a home office parent? Why or why not?

#2 Do I have my spouse's support with the ups and downs of home office parenting? How?

#3 If there were one thing I'd change about my spouse's response to/behavior around challenges that arise from home office parenting, what would it be?

#4 What can I do to better respect my spouse?

#5 What can I and my spouse do to step out of our daily roles and just enjoy each other?

CHAPTER SEVEN
Three Key Concepts

- As much as you respect your spouse's perspective and input, you will be respected. As much as you support your spouse's challenges, you will be supported.

- Aside from your own challenges and opportunities as a home office parent, you need to remember that your spouse is directly affected by the choices you make.

- Involve your spouse as more than household and childcare support in your business if you want him/her to be invested in supporting it and you.

CHAPTER SEVEN
Survival Strategies

- **Confront what's not working.** Be honest if there are repetitive negative situations that are driving you to wonder what life might be like if you were married to that thoughtful, flirty coffee barista down the street.

- **Make the unbreakable date.** Have at least one time each week set aside where you go out, avoid talking about the business and the kids, and just focus on each other. I find Friday evenings to be a perfectly-timed reprieve from the hectic pace of the week before.

- **Keep your spouse in the loop.** Make sure your spouse knows what is happening, or not happening, in the business and with the kids. Although you may sometimes feel like a dishrag that's been wrung out one too many times by the end of the day, be sure to take a few minutes and catch up.

- **What hidden talents can your spouse contribute to the business?** My husband, for example, is brilliant when it comes to estimates, profit margins and cost analysis. Sadly, I only discovered this last year when I bothered to ask him what he thought of a proposal I wasn't confident about. I knew he did that "at work" in his executive role, but it never occurred to me to ask him to put that talent to work in my business. Now, he manages that entire aspect of things, and, as a result, feels more invested in *my* work because it has become *our* work.

- **Evaluate risks together.** Younger entrepreneurs without families to feed can take incredible risks, because they are only gambling with their own livelihoods. You, on the other hand, have a spouse you respect and children to protect, so make risk-taking a team effort.

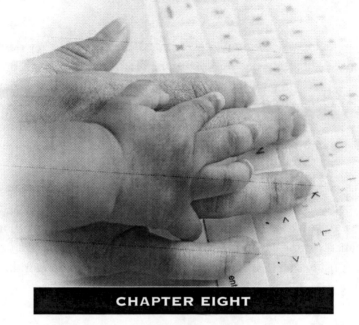

CHAPTER EIGHT

The Office Factor

A key component to being an effective home office parent is to have an effective home office setup for your business. One of the most common things that I've seen get in the way for home office parents is the feeling that their business materials and operations are spread all over the house, and that there is no central space out of which to work.

This typically occurs because the business endeavor starts out on a part-time basis, and until it feels like more than an income-generating hobby—and really starts to take off—it's difficult to carve out physical space for it to grow. The problem is that by the time the business starts to grow, there's no longer any down-time to create the space, so you're left to run around prying lollipop sticks off of your business plan and kicking toy trucks out of the way as you rehearse your presentation.

Many home office parents have confessed to me that they don't want to allocate space for something that might not work out. "Now, every time I walk past my 'sewing room,'" said one client, "I have to stop myself from thinking that a business used to live in there. Unless, and until, my new venture works out, I'm not rearranging so much as a chair."

That, of course, becomes a self-fulfilling prophecy, because if you don't believe your business will flourish, you're right. It can't grow into anything if you haven't put your belief and confidence behind it, and created space for it to develop. Henry Ford really said it all when he said, "If you think you can do a thing or think you can't do a thing, you're right."

Creating Office Space

Acknowledging your dual role as a home office parent begins with respecting your business as a meaningful, worthwhile endeavor. Meaningful, worthwhile endeavors require organized, dedicated space, which may be found in the guest bedroom, the rec room or even on the dining room table. Try to carve this out as far away from where most daily activity happens in your home. Wherever that space is, find it, claim it, and set it up as a center of operation.

Make it your own, and create a comfortable space that you look forward to working in. Maybe you have a great chair, or a CD player with all your favorite CDs within arms reach, or pictures of the kids on top of your monitor. Perhaps a scented candle will work for relaxation or your high school football trophy for inspiration.

Take ten minutes to organize the space before you close up each day, so that you start every morning fresh in a clear work space. With little ones afoot, the mornings will be hectic enough.

Business Tools

For an efficient office setup right from the start, ask yourself:

#1 What kind of computer system, software, and tech solutions are necessary to get started?

#2 What other type of equipment is needed?

#3 What tools are critical to my business operations other than a calculator to help count my profits?

#4 Is there any state or federal licensing required?

#5 What business entity paperwork is necessary, and how do I file it?

Support Team

What support team have you lined up for your business? If you haven't considered this yet, go out and establish relationships with an attorney, accountant, insurance agent, and maybe even a virtual assistant to help you manage growth and advise you on issues in which you have little expertise.

Also, be sure to research and sign up for accounts with service providers that will simplify your life, such as shipping resources, online fax services, and business post box providers (to keep your residential address private).

Goals & Planning

Now that you have the space to do it in, develop your goals and plans for this business. Create a business plan, a marketing plan, a financial plan, and a public relations plan. Just because you may be a one-man, home-based business, it doesn't mean you're not worthy of bigger business planning tools. Any entity, no matter how big or small, requires some sort of map so you don't get lost in the details.

Don't gloss over the goals either:

#1 Why are you starting this business?

#2 Can you sustain it from home?

#3 Do you hope to grow it slowly on the home front and then go wide open when your youngest child goes off to school?

#4 What are your expectations financially and otherwise?

#5 What if you get too successful too fast?

Business Documents

Take some time to create the document templates you'll be using in your business before you need them. Draft your proposals, contracts, and sales sheets ahead of time, so you can then just customize them for each client.

Also, figure out your rates and rate structures before you begin, if possible. Having these materials figured out and drafted from the beginning will cut down on frustration when the kids are glued to your lap.

An effective home office setup also shows your spouse and your kids that your business is a real entity with real components; they're reminded that your work is a big part of who you are, and that that part of you should be respected—along with the rest of you.

Some home office parents, like me, set up small desks in their offices for their kids. My daughters do their "work" on toy laptops, with princess pretend cell phones, and draft colorings galore—sometimes right alongside me. And, often, that's when I do my best work.

CHAPTER EIGHT
Success Exercises

#1 What does my ideal office space look like?

#2 How close can I come to creating my ideal space at home?

#3 What will I go out and purchase, or even find around the house, to create this space?

CHAPTER EIGHT
Three Key Concepts

• One of the most common things that I've seen get in the way for home office parents is the feeling that their business materials and operations are spread all over the house, and that there is no central space out of which to work.

• Acknowledging your dual role as a home office parent begins with respecting your business as a meaningful, worthwhile endeavor. Meaningful, worthwhile endeavors require organized, dedicated space, which may be found in the guest bedroom, the rec room or even on the dining room table.

• Don't think you'll create office space when the business starts to grow, because as soon as it does, there is no longer any downtime to create the space.

CHAPTER EIGHT
Survival Strategies

- **Claim your office.** Walk through each room of your house, and evaluate every potential corner where you can create your focused home office space. It may be as simple as reorganizing the furniture in the rec room or de-cluttering your existing arrangement.

- **Don't be afraid to take over the guest room.** You can leave the bed in there for Aunt Freda's annual weekend stay, but guest rooms are like little house museums; they look nice, but hardly anyone ever sleeps in them. Do the math...how often do guests occupy that room? Maybe 10 days per year? Weigh that against the five days a week you could be using that space (and writing it off on your taxes) and it's a no-brainer. And, it has a door you can close...a home office bonus!

- **Invest in the systems you'll need upfront.** From hardware to software to data backup and more, many home office parents wait until the business gets rolling before they buy the startup materials they need. This can cost you more than you would have spent in the first place, especially when your hard drive crashes and you have no backup recovery to rely on.

- **Surround yourself with motivation and positive images.** Pick a tropical screensaver so you can daydream about the beach when your computer nods off. If you love golf, decorate your office accordingly. If you still fear your judgmental Aunt Fern who told you you'd never amount to anything, don't hang her picture in here. This is your space.

- **Implement systems that will enable you to exit the office space.** Have a corded phone for important calls where you don't want to chance random static getting in the way, but have a cordless backup in case you hear a thud followed by screaming in another part of the house and you'd like to investigate. Better yet, invest in a headset that reduces background noise and has a mute function, so you can quickly and quietly explain to Johnny that his little sister was not meant to go in the dryer.

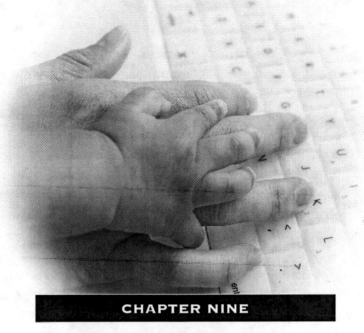

CHAPTER NINE

The Big Picture

Milk dumped on your keyboard. A trip to the ER when you're due in court. A screaming fit when you're on the phone with Client Numero Uno. Cheerios in your portfolio. A raging ear infection and 103° fever when you're on deadline. Insert your own private hellish experience here.

The daily pitfalls associated with home office parenting are many and varied. And I don't mean varied in a good way, as in "varied colors and sizes," but rather in a horrific "is this even anatomically possible?" kind of way. These moments are at best frustrating and at worst, and often, just plain gross. If such momentary challenges will drive you right into the arms of a qualified therapist, home office parenting may not be for you.

Home office parenting takes a strong stomach and a big picture mentality. Because, with challenges like these that befall all parents, you have to run a functional business on top of it all...typically down the hall from where this freak show is audibly taking place.

Try not to let these daily "opportunities for problem-solving" get you stuck, and go wide open with your vision. Big picture thinking is absolutely critical to home office parenting success. The balance between these two key roles you've taken on can only occur once you understand and accept that the likelihood that your day will go as planned is, well, unlikely.

But here's the big picture. You don't *have* to be at home with your kids. You *choose* to be at home with your kids. You *get* to be at home with your kids. So if one more juice spill threatens to send you right over the edge, remember the mom who's crying as she sits in traffic, missing her kids, worrying that the caregiver will look away at precisely the wrong moment. Or the Dad who has to leave for work before the kids get up and who doesn't get home until after they've gone to bed. Remember that many are the parents who have to work outside of the home who would gladly switch places with you.

The stress can be mind-numbing, but the payoff is huge. You see them roll over, crawl, and take that shaky first step. When they say "Dada" for the first time, you're there to hear it. You are on-site for the sheer victory and accomplishment on their faces when they achieve potty training success.

You are there when they are left out of a game during a play date. You are there when they fall down and need band-aids, and there when they just need you to say "there-there." And you are there when they can't get the stupid shapes in the stupid holes in the stupid box.

Through all of this, you have the opportunity to let them know that they matter so much to you that you made this not-always-easy choice to see them through this thing called *The First Five Years of Your Life*. There is great self-esteem that is inevitably built when a child feels seen and heard and valued.

When a discussion about a national or global problem comes up, such as world hunger or violent crime, I often hear the same sentiment: "I'm only one person. What am I going to do about it that would change anything?"

In being home office parents, that's what we can do. We can impart problem-solving skills, respectful guidance about how to treat other people, and one-on-one, focused time so that our kids feel ten feet tall in our eyes. We can show them balanced grown-ups who are fulfilled by both their work and their families, teaching them that life doesn't require a choice between the two.

By cultivating really decent human beings and sending them out into the world, we affect change. Good and needed change. Mahatma Gandhi encouraged us to "be the change you want to see in the world." So be the parent that raises the child that has the tools to be the change we want to see in the world.

We as home office parents are also blessed to have a marketable skill or product that makes entrepreneurship possible. Many people want the freedom and flexibility that comes with self-employment, but not all of them are able to create a sustainable business operation from a home-based office.

Like two sides of a well-flipped coin, home office parenting consistently involves the challenge on one side, and the gift on the other. Maybe little Matthew's recent super-human, lightning-fast climb to the highest shelf where you keep the cleaning products was a challenge to deal with while you were trying to pitch a reporter, but you were there to make sure he didn't plummet to the ground or ingest the stove cleaner—and therein lies the gift.

Isabella may have proved quite the challenge when she felt compelled to rip her little brother's bear from his arms, thus alerting you and your client that a grievous wrong had been done unto him...with a sound that sent you in for a hearing aid check. But the gift in there is that you had an opportunity to confront the behavior, talk to Isabella about how and why we respect people, and teach her about the importance of an apology.

Remember that it's *your* big picture, not someone else's. It's your vision and your approach to success, so establish parameters that honor the way you want to work and live. Develop your business strategy based on this personal vision, because this is work and life on your terms.

Keep flexibility in mind when you're trying to reach big picture objectives, and remember that it's perfectly OK to renegotiate and change your business plan, or the day's plan, as needed.

The reality of your life is that your computer will crash and your kids will get the flu. It's important to have a support team and safety net in place for unforeseen obstacles in realizing that big picture of yours, so line up resources before you need them. For those crises that bring everything to a screeching halt, keep a tech guru and accounting help on the speed dial. Try to have at least one family member or family friend in queue for emergencies, and guard your spouse's personal and sick days with vigilance.

So, here's my big, overall, been-there-done-that coping strategy and advice: hang in there and embrace the insanity. Your kids will turn five eventually, and they will have to attend school— by law. Once they're gone for eight hours a day, you'll have more time to grow your then-established business than you ever thought possible. And surprisingly, the peace and quiet you've craved for years may feel unexpectedly empty and a little too still.

Or, you may just dance around the office in your underwear, secure and celebratory in the fact that the only random shouts of boisterous glee are coming from you.

CHAPTER NINE
Success Exercises

#1 Describe your "big picture."

#2 What resources do I have lined up in case of emergencies, for both the business and the kids?

#3 What was my worst moment as a home office parent?

#4 What was my best moment as a home office parent?

#5 Who can I lean on when I lose sight of the big picture?

#6 Who will support me and help me to re-focus on the tougher days?

CHAPTER NINE
Three Key Concepts

- Here's the big picture: you don't *have* to be at home with your kids. You *choose* to be at home with your kids. You *get* to be at home with your kids. You have the opportunity to let them know that they matter so much to you that you have made this not-always-easy choice to see them through this thing called *The First Five Years of Your Life*. There is great self-esteem that is inevitably built when a child feels seen and heard and valued.

- We can impart problem-solving skills, respectful guidance about how to treat other people, and one-on-one, focused time so that our kids feel ten feet tall in our eyes. We can show them balanced grown-ups who are fulfilled by both their work and their families, teaching them that life doesn't require a choice between the two.

- Remember that it's your big picture, not someone else's. It's your vision and your approach to success, so establish parameters that honor the way you want to work and live. Develop your business strategy based on this personal vision, because this is work and life on your terms.

CHAPTER NINE
Survival Strategies

- **This too shall pass.** With each frustrating moment you experience, confront the temporary nature of the frustration. If frustration is becoming a lifestyle, however, then it's time to action plan a more healthy approach to daily home office parenting.

- **Adopt flexibility as a permanent mindset.** Being able to roll with it and accept that things will often not go as planned is part and parcel of successful home office parenting. If you have a tight or controlling grip on the way you feel things have to be, home office parenting will be a tougher ride for you. Try to let go of your inner control freak.

- **Celebrate the victories.** Keep a list of the day's accomplishments in front of you, and when you finish something, jot it down. Home office parents are spread pretty thin, so it can sometimes feel like nothing ever really gets done. Having written proof to the contrary helps to keep you going.

- **Outsource for a better bigger picture.** Home office parents understand that they have to leverage their time very carefully, so they truly appreciate the value of outsourcing. Visit a meal preparation service like Dream Dinners® and knock out a month's worth of meals in two hours. Have a cleaning service come in once every other week for hygiene purposes. Let a virtual assistant manage the business details that don't require your personal attention. While these may at first feel like luxuries, when you do the math, you find they really aren't. For every hour you save not having to prepare meals or mow the lawn, that's a potential billable hour. If you bill more per hour than you're paying out, you're profiting already. Outsourcing saves me no less than 60 hours—and those are billable hours—per month.

- **Own your vision.** Don't try to set up a home office parenting rhythm that makes sense on paper or that might work for someone else; set one up that works for the individual needs of you and your family.

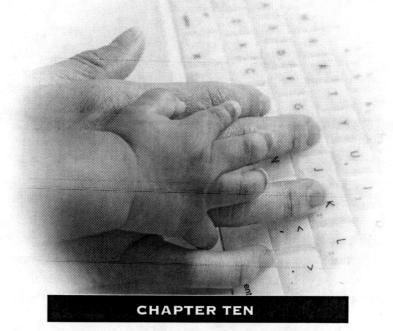

CHAPTER TEN

You Are an Enigma

e·nig·ma (Ã nig/ÆmÃ), *n., pl.* -mas, -ma·ta (-mÃ tÃ).
1. a puzzling or inexplicable occurrence or situation
2. a person of puzzling or contradictory character

Understand that you will probably only be fully understood by other home office parents and those that are married to such people. Your family and friends will try to get it because they love you, but they can't fully grasp the complexities and the clash of responsibilities involved in being a home office parent—and until I lived it, neither could I.

Some will think you have it easy and can lounge by the pool with the kids if you so choose. Although anyone who thinks you can lounge by the pool with a one- and a four-year old has clearly never been to a pool with small children. By the time you get the sunscreen on every conceivable part of their bodies, blow up the floaties, and make sure all heads are above water, you're exhausted and the sun has set. But I digress…

Some will think you work too much, so why bother being at home? If you're always on deadline and taking meetings and having help come in, where does the "parenting" part come in?

Some will think your business is really just a fancy hobby with business cards, because "real" businesses typically exist in commercial spaces, not dining rooms. But what they don't appreciate is that with the boon of the Internet, and entrepreneurs everywhere serving up virtual staffing solutions, commercial space is simply a needless overhead expense for many businesses.

Some will not understand that your spouse may have to start Job #2 during the evenings and on weekends, washing up and tucking in little bodies, running the dishwasher and mowing the lawn, because you have only that uninterrupted time to work in your office. If one of the "some" is your spouse, it's time for a talk.

Some will think you are really a stay-at-home-parent who dabbles in business when it's convenient. They will not understand how busy you can sometimes be, and that you can't always meet at the park for a play date or go to the zoo for the day because you really do have to work. Wherever there's a nap or another crack through which you can slide some office productivity, you jump on it.

Your friends and family need to understand that you are not only running, but also building, a real-life business that has clients who need to have their calls and emails returned and who would like you to do what they've paid you to do. While many people confuse the two, there is a big difference between a stay-at-home-parent and a home-office parent. One is not better or worse than the other, but they are *very* different choices.

You will be judged, and you will at some point be criticized. But my Grandmother taught me how to handle this one many moons ago: "If they're talking about you," she said, "they're leaving somebody else alone."

The criticism might sound something like, "Who is she to think she can have it both ways? A real mother would focus on the needs of the children. She can work when they go off to school." Or, "What kind of a family man works out of the rec room? He must get his fair share of TV time." My question is, who are you to be judged by people who have not attempted what you have? Who have never had to balance what you do? Who have never dared to say, "I *can* live and work on my terms?"

And then, there are the *some* that you'll appreciate beyond measure. Some who will 100% believe in you, support you, offer unlimited help when you're struggling and take you out for dinner when you sign a big client. Those are the *some* to talk to, lean on and soak up.

If these people haven't fallen into your life by accident, go out and find them. Home office parents are all over the place. Network, ask colleagues, look for home-based business groups, and visit sites online to at least get some virtual support from a discussion board.

Even though many people in your life won't get it, give them points for trying. And avoid the urge to isolate because you feel as though no one understands your choice. Go find the people who do, because they need your support, too.

CHAPTER TEN
Success Exercises

#1 Who in my life doesn't understand my choice? What can I say to them to help them understand what they can say and do to help me?

#2 Do I have other home office parents in my network? If not, what am I going to do to find some?

#3 Name three people who support you and your creative approach to raising kids and profits under the same roof.

CHAPTER TEN
Three Key Concepts

- Understand that you will probably only be fully understood by other home office parents and those that are married to such people.

- While many people confuse the two, there is a big difference between a stay-at-home-parent and a home-office parent. One is not better or worse than the other, but they are very different choices.

- If entrepreneurial peers haven't fallen into your life by accident, go out and find them. Home office parents are all over the place.

CHAPTER TEN
Survival Strategies

- **Accept unsolicited advice graciously.** When well-meaning, non-home office parenting friends and relatives offer up opinions about how you can manage things more effectively, accept that they really are trying to help and haven't the first clue what you're dealing with. Smile and nod.

- **Create community with like-minded people.** Get some other home-office parents together and attempt lunch with little ones (so they can network too). Be sure to also carve out some adults-only time so you can support and empower each other in complete sentences, uninterrupted by a variety of high-pitched requests and ongoing hygiene issues.

- **Spread the wealth.** If you've carved out a great home-office parenting setup that really works for you, shout it out! Offer to speak at networking groups and share what you've learned on the journey. It's a great way to empower other home office parents while simultaneously getting great exposure for your business.

- **Remember that it is easier to follow than to lead.** When you step outside the traditional model of the way things have always been done, you are inevitably going to make people who subscribe to that model uncomfortable. Their discomfort will unfortunately often manifest as criticism, so try to remember that judgment is the hallmark of the insecure. Lead on!

- **Celebrate your incredible choice!** Home office parenting is truly a gift.

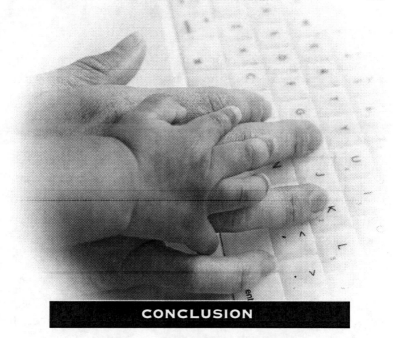

CONCLUSION

Profits & Playdoh & Peace...Oh My

When you flirt with the idea of running a business from home, it at first sounds like the perfect setup. No more commuting, day care, or dry cleaning would suit you just fine. But when you take a closer look at all of the issues and people involved in the decision to become a home office parent, you realize how much there is to consider. While this can feel overwhelming to say the least, the strong foundation you're now able to lay for a solid home office parenting endeavor will propel you toward the success you know is possible.

Through the exercises in each chapter, you've been able to think through challenges, opportunities, and resources you may not have fully examined before. You've taken the time to understand how you define things like success and balance, why prioritizing and setting boundaries is crucial to home office parenting success, and what kind of support and environment you need to clear the hurdles inherent to anything worth doing.

Once you have a clear picture of the *what* and the *why*, you can move forward with the *how*. In completing these chapter exercises, you have essentially created a road map for your home office parenting success story. And the beauty of a road map is you can refer to it when you stray off course, or choose an alternate route when you become more familiar with the terrain.

We entrepreneurs all strive for a profitable enterprise, but profit is more than a margin for the home office parent. Profit happens when both your life and your business are in balance. If one is picking up the tab for the other, profit doesn't exist.

Home office parenting is not always the perfect daily setup we once imagined, but it is definitely worth the journey. And, at the end of the day, as your children lay sleeping, your spouse is on the treadmill, and the computer screen blurs your vision, you can close the laptop knowing that you were more than a parent and more than a business owner today. You were a home office parent today, and your family and clients are better for it.

About the Author

 Jennifer Kalita has been a communications and business consultant, writer, speaker and strategist for more than a decade. She empowers entrepreneurs, home-based business owners, women in business, and baby boomers in transition to live a life *In Business and In Balance™*, and has educated thousands of entrepreneurs in all facets of business launch, development, and promotion.

Jennifer is the founder and CEO of *The Kalita Group* (www.thekalitagroup.com), an entrepreneurial services and resource company. Regularly interviewed by major media, you'll find her quoted in national publications from *Working Mother* magazine to the *L.A. Times*, as well as in online business communities such as *StartUpNation.com* and *EntrepreneurialConnection.com*.

Also a nationally-recognized 50+ market expert, Jennifer is the Entrepreneurial Columnist to the *National Association of Baby Boomer Women*; the Entrepreneurial Columnist to *Boomer Magazine*; and a contributing author and *Creating Boomer Buzz* PR columnist at *Second50Years.com*.

Jennifer has developed and taught teleseminars on a variety of marketing, public relations, management and growth topics for small business owners, and she has authored numerous e-books and business development programs for entrepreneurial success.

In addition to *The Home Office Parent: How to Raise Kids &* *Profits Under One Roof*, Jennifer also shares her success strategies for mom entrepreneurs as a contributing author to *The Business Mom Guide Book: More Life, Less Overwhelm for Mom Entrepreneurs*. In *Inspirations to Realizations, Volume 3*, she reveals her formula for living *In Business & In Balance*™.

A graduate of Loyola College in Maryland, Jennifer resides in the Washington, D.C. metropolitan area with her husband and two daughters.

It's not just a book…it's a community.

Introducing

The Home Office Parent Online Resource Center!

Get more home office parenting tools,
tips and resources online now at
www.TheHomeOfficeParent.com

Download templates for the success exercises, recommended
checklists and other strategies mentioned throughout *The
Home Office Parent*, and get access to exclusive community
resources.

- *Want to* start your own *Home Office Parent* networking
  group? We'll show you how.

- *Looking to* connect with other empowered home office
  parents across the globe? No problem.

- *Ready to* boost your bottom line with marketing and
  PR know-how? We've got the experts.

Log on today and empower yourself, your business
and your family at:
www.TheHomeOfficeParent.com

Printed in the United States
93862LV00001B/11/A

9 781932 279689